THE WORKBOOK ON
LOVING
THE
JESUS WAY

THE WORKBOOK ON
Loving
the
Jesus
Way

Maxie Dunnam

UPPER
ROOM BOOKS
NASHVILLE

THE WORKBOOK ON LOVING THE JESUS WAY
Copyright © 1995 by Maxie Dunnam. All rights reserved.

Unless otherwise indicated scripture quotations are from The New Revised Standard Version of the Bible, copyright © 1989 by the Division of Christian Education of the National Council of the Churches of Christ in the United States of America. Used by permission.

Scripture quotations designated RSV are from the Revised Standard Version of the Bible, copyrighted 1946, 1952, and © 1971 by the Division of Christian Education, National Council of the Churches of Christ in the United States of America, and are used by permission.

Scripture quotations designated PHILLIPS are from THE NEW TESTAMENT IN MODERN ENGLISH by J. B. Phillips 1958. Used by permission of The Macmillan Company.

Scripture quotations designated NKJV are from The New King James Version. Copyright © 1979, 1980, 1982, Thomas Nelson, Inc.

The designation KJV is used throughout this book to identify quotations from the King James Version of the Bible.

Scripture quotations designated TEV are from the *Good News Bible*, The Bible in Today's English Version—Old Testament: Copyright © American Bible Society 1976; New Testament: Copyright © American Bible Society 1966, 1971, 1976.

All scripture quotations designated JB are from THE JERUSALEM BIBLE, published and copyright 1966, 1967, and 1968 by Darton, Longman & Todd Ltd. and Doubleday & Co., Inc., and are used by permission of the publishers.

All scripture quotations designated NJB are from THE NEW JERUSALEM BIBLE, published and copyright 1985 by Darton, Longman & Todd Ltd. and Doubleday & Co., Inc., and are used by permission of the publishers.

Scripture quotations designated NIV are from the *Holy Bible, New International Version*. Copyright © 1973, 1978, 1984 International Bible Society. Used by permission of Zondervan Bible Publishers.

Scripture quotations designated NEB are from *The New English Bible*. © The Delegates of Oxford University Press and The Syndics of the Cambridge University Press 1961, 1970. Reprinted with permission.

The publisher gratefully acknowledges permission to reproduce the following copyrighted material:

"Minnie Remembers" by Donna Swanson from *Mind Song*. For reprints contact the author at R. 1, Box 159, Williamsport, IN 47993.

Excerpts from "How Many Times Do You Take the Prodigal Back?" used by permission of William A. Ritter.

Cover design: John Robinson
Cover photograph: Leo de Wys/Steve Vidler
Second printing: March 1996 (10)
ISBN: 0-8358-0729-0

Printed in the United States of America

From the time that it was shown I desired often to know what was our Lord's meaning. And fifteen years after and more, I was answered in inward understanding, saying, "Would you know your Lord's meaning in this? Learn it well. Love was his meaning. Who showed it you? Love. What did he show you? Love. Why did he show you? For love. Hold fast to this, and you shall learn and know more about love, but you will never need to know or understand about anything else for ever and ever." Thus did I learn that love was our Lord's meaning.

Julian of Norwich

CONTENTS

INTRODUCTION

THERE WAS A TIME WHEN NATIVE AMERICANS communicated by drums and smoke signals. Years ago, when the atomic bomb was being tested out on the flats of Nevada, a cartoon pictured some tribesmen. They were looking across the barren wastes—the spacious flats—when on the horizon the mushroom smoke cloud of an atomic explosion rose dramatically. As they looked in wonder—never having seen smoke like this—one said to the other, "I wish *I* had said that!"

Many a poet, prosewriter, essayist, scholar, preacher, and singer, reading Paul's magnificent hymn of love in 1 Corinthians 13, has felt, though perhaps not verbalizing it, "I wish I had said that." Reading this passage, we, too, want to exclaim, "Aha! That's it!"

This is Paul's exposition of love, expressed poetically but leaving nothing out. Our souls resonate with it because it is truth we have experienced, or need desperately to experience. With extraordinary understanding and pristine clarity, with unmuddied sensitivity and spiritual depth, Paul has mined the very essence of the Christian gospel. It is no wonder that whenever Christians gather to worship, wherever the gospel is proclaimed, 1 Corinthians 13 is known and loved.

We're going to spend the next seven weeks with this beloved passage. This is Paul's exposition of the meaning of *agape*, the New Testament word for Christian love. Though we will call on other passages of scripture, this chapter will be the centerpiece for our journey in *Loving the Jesus Way*.

The essence of Jesus' person and ministry was love. Julian of Norwich gave powerful witness to this.

From the time that it was shown I desired often to know what was our Lord's meaning. And fifteen years after and more, I was answered in inward understanding, saying, "Would you know your Lord's meaning in this? Learn it well. Love was his

9

meaning. Who showed it you? Love. What did he show you? Love. Why did he show you? For love. Hold fast to this, and you shall learn and know more about love, but you will never need to know or understand about anything else for ever and ever." Thus did I learn that love was our Lord's meaning.

And so I saw full surely that before ever God made us, he loved us. And this love was never quenched nor ever shall be. And in this love he has done all his works, and in this love he has made all things profitable to us, and in this love our life is everlasting. In our making we had beginning, but the love in which he made us was in him from without beginning, in which love we have our beginning.

Certainly we will not say the last word about love. But we will say enough to engage ourselves in loving. If you follow the plan and the suggestions, the next seven weeks will put you on a love-path from which, I pray, you will never detour.

Let's look at the process of this workbook. It is simple, but over and over again it has proven effective.

I have found in my many years of teaching and ministry with small groups that a six- to eight-week period for a group study is the most manageable and effective. I also have learned that persons can best appropriate content and truth in small doses. This is why I have organized the material in segments to be read daily.

The plan for this workbook is the same as for the previous ones I have written. It calls for a seven-week commitment. You are asked to give thirty minutes each day to learn about and appropriate ideals and disciplines for your transformation and growth. For most persons, the thirty minutes will come at the beginning of the day. If it is not possible for you to give the time at the beginning of the day, do it whenever the time is available, but do it regularly. The purpose of this spiritual journey must not be forgotten: to incorporate the content into your daily life.

Although this is an individual journey, my hope is that you will share it with some fellow pilgrims with whom you will meet together once a week during the seven weeks of the study.

The workbook is arranged in seven major divisions, each designed to guide you for one week. These divisions contain seven sections, one for each day of the week. Each day will have three major aspects: reading about the discipline, reflecting and recording ideas and thoughts about the material and your own journey, and finally, giving some practical suggestions for incorporating ideas from the reading material into your daily life.

In each day's section, you will read about common problems and needs and/or possibilities for transformation and direction for growth. The readings are not lengthy, but will link you with the challenges of your recovery and growth—problems, experiences, relationships, and situations with which we all must cope. Included in each reading will be portions of scripture, the basic resource for Christian discipline and living. Quotations from most sources other than scripture are followed by the author's name and the page number on which each quote can be found. These citations are keyed to the Notes section at the back of the workbook, where you will find a complete bibliography should you wish to read certain works more fully.

Throughout the workbook you will see the symbol ♥. When you come to this symbol, *please stop*. Do not read any further. Think and reflect as you are requested to do in order to internalize the ideas being shared or the experience reflected upon.

Reflecting and Recording

After the reading each day, there will be a time for reflecting and recording. This dimension calls you to record some of your reflections. The degree of meaning you receive from this workbook is largely dependent upon your faithfulness to its practice. You may be unable on a particular day to do precisely what is requested. If so, then simply record that fact and make a note of why you can't follow through. This may give you some insight about yourself and help you to grow.

Also, on some days there may be more suggestions than you can deal with in the time you have. Do what is most meaningful for you, and do not feel guilty.

The emphasis in this workbook is upon growth, not perfection. Don't feel guilty if you do not follow the pattern of the days exactly. Follow the content and direction seriously, but not slavishly.

Finally, always remember that this is a personal pilgrimage. What you write in your personal workbook is your private property. You may not wish to share it with anyone. For this reason, no two people should attempt to share the same workbook. The importance of what you write is not what it may mean to someone else, but what it means to you. Writing, even if it is only brief notes or single-word reminders, helps us clarify our thoughts and feelings.

As indicated earlier, there will be places where you will come to this sign ♥. Please do not move on in your reading until you spend time reflecting as suggested. The significance of the reflecting and recording dimension will grow as you move along. Even beyond the seven weeks, you will find meaning in looking back at what you wrote on a particular day in response to a particular situation.

Sharing with Others

John Wesley believed that Christian "conferencing" was a means of grace for Christians. By Christian conferencing he simply meant Christians sharing intentionally their Christian experience and understanding in deliberate and serious conversation. He designed the "class meeting" as a vehicle for this discipline. In such a fellowship of Christian conversation and shared life, "one loving heart sets another on fire." The content and dynamic of this workbook will be more meaningful if you share it with others. As you share with others your own insight will be sharpened. Others will become a source of encouragement and a catalyst for change. Your weekly gathering can be that kind of means of grace. A guide for group sharing is included in the text at the end of each week.

If this is a group venture, all persons should begin their personal involvement with the workbook on the same day, so that when you come together to share as a group, you all will have been dealing with the same material and will be at the same place in the text. It will be helpful if you have an initial get-acquainted group meeting to begin the adventure. A guide for this meeting is provided in this introduction.

Group sessions for this workbook are designed to last one and one-half hours (with the exception of the initial meeting). Those sharing in the group should covenant to attend all sessions unless an emergency prevents attendance. There will be seven weekly sessions in addition to this first get-together time.

A group consisting of eight to twelve members is about the right size. Larger numbers will tend to limit individual involvement.

One person may provide the leadership for the entire seven weeks, or leaders may be assigned from week to week. The leader's task is to:

   1. Read the directions and determine ahead of time how to handle

the session. It may not be possible to use all the suggestions for sharing and praying together. Feel free to select those you think will be most meaningful and those for which you have adequate time.

2. Model a style of openness, honesty, and warmth. A leader should not ask others to share what he or she is not willing to share. Usually the leader should be the first to share, especially as it relates to personal experiences.

3. Moderate the discussion.

4. Encourage reluctant members to participate, and try to prevent the same few persons from doing all the talking.

5. Keep the sharing centered in personal experience, rather than academic debate.

6. Honor the time schedule. If it appears necessary to go longer than one and one-half hours, the leader should get consensus for continuing another twenty or thirty minutes.

7. See that the meeting time and place are known by all, especially if meetings are held in different homes.

8. Make sure that the necessary materials for meetings are available and that the meeting room is arranged ahead of time.

It is a good idea for weekly meetings to be held in the homes of the participants. (Hosts or hostesses should make sure there are as few interruptions as possible from children, telephone, pets, and so forth.) If the meetings are held in a church they should be in an informal setting. Participants are asked to dress casually, to be comfortable and relaxed.

If refreshments are served, they should come *after* the formal meeting. In this way, those who wish to stay longer for informal discussion may do so, while those who need to keep to the specific time schedule will be free to leave, but will get the full value of the meeting time.

Suggestions for Initial Get-Acquainted Meeting

Since the initial meeting is for the purpose of getting acquainted and beginning the shared pilgrimage, here is a good way to get started.

1. Have each person in the group give his or her full name and the name by which each wishes to be called. Do away with titles. Address every person by his or her first name or nickname. If name tags are needed, provide them. Each person should make a

list of the names somewhere in his or her workbook.

2. Let each person in the group share one of the happiest, most exciting, or most meaningful experiences he or she has had during the past three or four weeks. After everyone has shared in this way, let the entire group sing the Doxology or a chorus of praise.

3. After this experience of happy sharing, ask each person who will to share his or her expectation of this workbook study. Why did he or she become a part of it? What does each expect to gain from it? What are the reservations?

4. The leader should now review the introduction to the workbook and ask if there are questions about directions and procedures. (The leader should have read the introduction prior to the meeting.) If persons have not received copies of the workbook, the books should be handed out now. Remember that every person must have his or her own workbook.

5. **DAY ONE** in the workbook is the day following this initial meeting, and the next meeting should be held on **DAY SEVEN** of the first week. If a group must choose a weekly meeting time other than seven days from this initial session, the reading assignment should be adjusted so that the weekly meetings are always on **DAY SEVEN**, and **DAY ONE** is always the day following a weekly meeting.

6. Nothing binds members together more than praying for one another. The leader should encourage each participant to write the names of persons in the group in his or her workbook, and commit to praying for them by name daily throughout the seven weeks.

7. After checking to see that everyone knows the time and place of the next meeting, the leader should close with a prayer, thanking God for each person in the group, for the opportunity for growth, and for the possibility of growing in the spiritual disciplines.

One final note: If someone in the group has an instant or Polaroid camera, ask him or her to bring it to the group meeting the next week. Be prepared to take a picture of each person in the group to be used as an aid to prayer.

WEEK ONE

Love
Was His
Meaning

"ABIDE IN MY LOVE"

IN THE INTRODUCTION TO THE WORKBOOK, on page 9, I share a long quote of Julian of Norwich. If you did not read it, please do so now. (When you come to this sign ♥, please do not move on until you follow the directions suggested.)

Julian of Norwich is one of that great galaxy of souls we call "giants of the spiritual life." For years in her spiritual quest, she had struggled with the question, what was Jesus all about? "What was our Lord's meaning?" she asked.

The answer finally came. "Would you know your Lord's meaning in this? Learn it well. Love was his meaning."

Julian had been struggling over particular circumstances and issues in her life. But that which came *uniquely* to her, is true *in general* for all of us, and *in particular* for each of us. Jesus, himself, says so.

As the Father has loved me, so I have loved you; abide in my love. If you keep my commandments, you will abide in my love, just as I have kept my Father's commandments and abide in his love. I have said these things to you so that my joy may be in you, and that your joy may be complete.

This is my commandment, that you love one another as I have loved you. No one has greater love than this, to lay down one's life for one's friends. You are my friends if you do what I command you. I do not call you servants any longer, because the servant does not know what the master is doing; but I have called you friends because I have made known to you everything that I have heard from my Father.

—John 15:9-15

This word of Jesus comes immediately after his use of the beautiful metaphor of the vine and the branches. With that metaphor, he tells us who he is in relation to the Father: "I am the true vine, and my Father is the vinegrower" (verse 1). Then he tells us who we are in relation to him: "I am the vine, you are the branches" (verse 5).

The symbolism is rich and powerfully suggestive:

Abide in me as I abide in you. Just as the branch cannot bear fruit by itself unless it abides in the vine, neither can you unless you abide in me. I am the vine, you are the branches. Those who abide in me and I in them bear much fruit, because apart from me you can do nothing. Whoever does not abide in me is thrown away like a branch and withers.

—John 15:4-6*a*

Jesus closes this teaching about the relationship between himself and the Father, and between us and him, with a challenging word: "My Father is glorified by this, that you bear much fruit and become my disciples" (John 15:8). He then moves to the passage printed above, verses 9-15.

It could not be clearer. To be a Christian is to abide in Christ. To abide in Christ is to abide in love. Dame Julian was right: *Love was his meaning*.

A pastor in Dallas recalled a powerful story about a famous plastic surgeon. A woman came to see him one day. "It's my husband," she said. "He has been injured in a fire. He tried to save his parents from a burning house but he couldn't get to them. They were both killed. His face was burned and disfigured, and he has quit on life. He has gone into hiding and won't let anyone see him, not even me. He has shut me and everyone out." "Don't worry," the doctor responded, "I can fix him. With the great advances we've made in plastic surgery in recent years, I can restore his face."

"But that's just it," said the woman. "He won't let anyone help him. He thinks God did this to punish him because he didn't save his parents." Then came her shocking words. "I want you to disfigure my face so I can be like him! If I can share in his pain, maybe then he will let me back into his life. I love him so much. I want to be with him. And if that's what it takes, that's what I want to do."

Of course, the plastic surgeon would not agree. Moved deeply by the wife's determined and total love, with the wife's permission, he went to the man's room and knocked, but there was no answer. He then said loudly through the door, "I know you are in there and I know you can hear me. I'm a plastic surgeon, and I want you to know that I can restore your face."

No response. The doctor pleaded, "Please come out and let me help you." Still no answer. Then, still speaking through the door, the doctor told the man what his wife was asking him to do. "She wants me to disfigure her face. She wants me to make her face like yours in the hope that then you will let her back into your life. That's how much she loves you. That's how much she wants to help you!"

There was a brief moment of silence. Then, ever so slowly, the door knob began to turn . . . and the disfigured man came out to make a new beginning and to find a new life. By her love he was set free, brought out of hiding, and given a new start.

In the John passage printed above, Jesus said, "No one has greater love than this, to lay down one's life for one's friends" (verse 13). Jesus went on to do just that—to lay down his life for us. *Love was his meaning.*

Reflecting and Recording

The stories of the woman's love for her husband and of Jesus dying on the cross for us are overwhelming. Stories like that don't happen every day. But love does happen every day. Sit for a while and reflect on the love you have received and the opportunities you have had to give love during the past week.

Offer a prayer of thanksgiving for the love of Jesus in your life and for the people who love you.

During the Day
Look closely at life today and pay attention to love.

Day Two

JESUS *WAS* LOVE

I HAD JUST BEEN ELECTED PRESIDENT of Asbury Theological Seminary. This was an expression of vocation I had never considered. God acts in surprising ways. Though we didn't understand, and though it was the most painful decision we have ever made, Jerry (my wife) and I were convinced that this was God's leading.

This conviction of God's leading enabled me to respond to the call; it did not, however, relieve my fear and deep feelings of inadequacy. I had been a member of an academic community only as a student, and I had no "terminal" degree in any academic discipline. Because of my cultural and educational background, I always felt that my formal education was limited. Satan uses the mind to work strange tricks on us. More often than not, I thought my peers were smarter than I, and I was intimidated by the academic community.

Now, here I was—thrust into such a community as president, with every faculty member more formally educated than I.

One of the primary responsibilities of a leader is to set the vision and communicate that vision, both to the "inside" community and to "the world." In the case of my new responsibility, this was the beginning task. People, especially faculty, were asking, "What's he going to do?" "What are his big ideas about theological education?" "Where will he take the seminary?"

One day, after a long period of conversation, anguishing, prayer, and wrestling about this issue and my beginning ministry at the seminary, Jerry shared my struggle with a minister friend. Everything centered around my feelings of inadequacy and my desperate desire to communicate a calling and a vision that I felt deeply, but could not articulate. Our friend said a shocking thing: "Ah, Jerry, he *is* the vision."

He went on to talk about how my forty years of experience in ministry, especially the last twelve years as pastor of a growing, vital congregation where mission and ministry had transformed lives and impacted the city, could inform the preparation of young men and women for ministry in the church.

His word, though shocking, and though it could come off as arrogant if I took it the wrong way, has impacted my thinking and action. It is a challenging word that gets at the core of Christianity, especially the heart of the Christian way: *love*.

The greatest verbal statements about love in the New Testament were not spoken by Jesus. They come from the pen of Paul, particularly his hymn of love, 1 Corinthians 13. Jesus did not have to speak, because he *was* it. *He was love.*

Every action, every word, every thought that came from Jesus was a demonstration of love. You don't have to verbalize if all that you are speaks its meaning. One particular incident in Jesus' life makes the case.

> Early in the morning he came again to the temple. All the people came to him and he sat down and began to teach them. The scribes and the Pharisees brought a woman who had been caught in adultery; and making her stand before all of them, they said to him, "Teacher, this woman was caught in the very act of committing adultery. Now in the law Moses commanded us to stone such women. Now what do you say?" They said this to test him, so that they might have some charge to bring against him. Jesus bent down and wrote with his finger on the ground. When they kept on questioning him, he straightened up and said to them, "Let anyone among you who is without sin be the first to throw a stone at her." And once again he bent down and wrote on the ground. When they heard it, they went away, one by one, beginning with the elders; and Jesus was left alone with the woman standing before him. Jesus straightened up and said to her, "Woman, where are they? Has no one condemned you?" She said, "No one, sir." And Jesus said, "Neither do I condemn you. Go your way, and from now on do not sin again."
>
> —John 8:2-11

Persons who live like Jesus don't have to speak and/or write about love; you just look at them and get the message.

Reflecting and Recording

Write in this blank space the name of a person who, more than anyone you know, is a living expression of love.

What is there in the life of this person that is not present in your own life? Make some notes.

Spend some time reflecting on how you might make your daily living a clearer expression of love.

During the Day

Continue to look closely at life today, and pay attention to love.

Day Three

LOVE IS THE GREATEST

And now faith, hope, and love, abide, these three; but the greatest of these is love.

—1 Corinthians 13:13

AUGUSTINE ASKED, "WHERE LOVE IS, what can be wanting? Where it is not, what can possibly be profitable?"

In that delightful book, *Mister God, This Is Anna*, the little girl Anna encounters the Vicar one day in the High Street. The conversation goes something like this:

Parson: Do you believe in God?
Anna: Yes.
Parson: Do you know what God is?
Anna: Yes.
Parson: What is God then?
Anna: He's God!
Parson: Do you go to church?
Anna: No.
Parson: Why not?
Anna: Because I know it all!
Parson: What do you know?
Anna: I know to love Mister God and to love people and cats and dogs and spiders and flowers and trees [the catalogue went on] with all of me.

Fynn comments, "There's nothing much you can do in the face of that kind of accusation. . . . Anna had bypassed all the non-essentials and distilled centuries of learning into one sentence: 'And God said love me, love them, and love it, and don't forget to love yourself'" (Fynn, p. 19).

The most magnificent moments in our individual lives come when the primacy of love is experienced and celebrated. The greatest chapters in the history of the Christian church have nearly always included the rediscovery of the centrality of love in the gospel and the primacy of love in the faith community.

Reflecting and Recording
Spend a few minutes pondering Augustine's word: "Where love is, what can be wanting? Where it is not, what can possibly be profitable?"

During the Day
Throughout the day, make a mental note of relationships, situations, and occasions where love is and where love is not. Reflect on what is present, what is missing, and what is the emotional/spiritual tone.

Day Four

ENERGIZED GOODWILL

WHILE 1 CORINTHIANS 13 IS PAUL'S incomparable poetic expression of love, he was always calling people to love. He never left any doubt about the practical meaning of love. Here is an example.

> Therefore, as the elect of God, holy and beloved, put on tender mercies, kindness, humility, meekness, longsuffering; bearing with one another, and forgiving one another, if anyone has a complaint against another; even as Christ forgave you, so you also must do.
>
> But above all these things put on love, which is the bond of perfection. And let the peace of God rule in your hearts, to which also you were called in one body; and be thankful.
>
> Let the word of Christ dwell in you richly in all wisdom, teaching and admonishing one another in psalms and hymns and spiritual songs, singing with grace in your hearts to the Lord.
>
> And whatever you do in word or deed, do all in the name of the Lord Jesus, giving thanks to God the Father through Him.
> —Colossians 3:12-17, NKJV

Years ago, Senator Paul Douglas offered this marvelous definition of love: "What the world needs most is love, or energized goodwill, which if given a chance and practiced with devotion can in most cases melt antagonisms and reconcile opposites" (McConnell, 370).

What a fitting description of love . . . "energized goodwill." It certainly expresses the style of Jesus' expression of love. Think about it.

> Love with energy is sometimes the only way in which we can cope with some persons or harsh realities. Love is the only force strong enough to break walls that divide persons. It is the goodwill whereby things can change. God energized love is the gift of Jesus to humanity. John Wesley writes of the importance of love in this way: "Let love not visit you as a transient guest,

but be the constant temper of your soul. . . . See that your heart is filled at all times and on all occasions with real undissembled benevolence. Let it pant in your heart, let it sparkle in your eyes, let it shine in your actions. Whenever you open your lips let it be with love; and let there be on your tongue the law of kindness" (McConnell, 370).

How desperately we need to accept Wesley's admonition. We see the problem in blatant expressions on television—Iraqi and Iranian children, and Muslim children in other lands, are taught to hate Americans, "the Great Satan."

But the shoe also fits our foot. Think about the way we are taught in subtle ways to hate. The terms *Arab* and *terrorist* are almost always used together, suggesting that all Arabs are terrorists. A Jordanian ambassador to the United States struck a nerve when he pointed out that when one American kills another, we don't refer to that person as the "Christian murderer." Why do we tar the world's 200 million Arabs and one billion Muslims with the prejudiced stereotype, "terrorist"? (Kamal, February 16, 1987).

Reflecting and Recording

Recall your most recent experience of love as "energized goodwill." Make some notes describing that experience here.

Can you recall a close-to-home experience in which you have labeled people with stereotypes which cultivate suspicion, fear, or even hatred, rather than "energized goodwill"? Reflect on that experience and how you identified with it.

During the Day

Paul admonished us to "clothe [ourselves] with love, which binds everything together in perfect harmony." Seek to live this day "clothed in love."

Day Five

GOD IS LOVE

Beloved, let us love one another, because love is from God; everyone who loves is born of God and knows God. Whoever does not love does not know God, for God is love. God's love was revealed among us in this way: God sent his only Son into the world so that we might live through him. In this is love, not that we loved God but that he loved us and sent his Son to be the atoning sacrifice for our sins. Beloved, since God loved us so much, we also ought to love one another.

—1 John 4:7-11

ONE OF THE MOST SUCCINCT and striking statements in the New Testament is the word of John from this passage: "God is love." If this is true, then we can't understand the nature of love without understanding the nature of God. For the Christian, our knowledge of God is connected with our knowledge of Jesus Christ. God has revealed God's self to us in Jesus.

We don't begin our exploration of love by thinking of love as a *principle*. To do so—to see love as a principle—leads to distortions either in the rigorous legalistic sense or in the indulgent hedonistic sense. We know what the love of God is when we see the way God acts. The clearest expression of God's action is in Jesus Christ.

Dr. Dand Rahbar, a highly intelligent Moslem, wrote to his Moslem friends after his conversion to Christ.

In our search for the truly worshipable we must look in human history for a man who loved, who lived humbly like the poorest, who was perfectly innocent and sinless, who was tortured and humiliated in literally the worst manner and who declared his continued transparent love for those who had inflicted the worst of injuries upon him. If we do find such a man, he must be the Creator-God himself. For if the Creator-God himself is not that supremely suffering and loving man, then the Creator-God is provenly inferior to that man. And this cannot be. Such a man did live on earth . . . his name was Jesus. . . . When I read the New Testament and discovered how Jesus loved and forgave his killers from the Cross, I could not fail to recognise that the love He had for men is the only kind of love worthy of the Eternal God (Harper, 211).

God is love. We see the nature and shape of that love in Jesus Christ.

Reflecting and Recording

The key to understanding and experiencing love, as we are exploring love in this workbook, is in the crucifixion of Jesus Christ. The Cross is the expression of the eternal love of God. It was and is a world-changing event.

A poster pictures Jesus hanging on a cross, his arms outstretched on the crossbeam, and his hands violently nailed down. The words beneath the picture say, "I asked Jesus how much He loved me. He stretched out His arms and said, 'This much.'"

Spend a few minutes in quiet reflection on what the Cross means to you. What is God saying to you in the Cross?

During the Day

Look for signs of Cross-love today.

Day Six

LOVE IS THE HEARTBEAT OF GOD

You have heard that it was said, "Love your friends, hate your enemies." But now I tell you: Love your enemies and pray for those who persecute you, so that you become the sons of your Father in Heaven. For He makes the sun to shine on bad and good people alike, and gives rain to those who do good and to those who do evil. Why should God reward you if you love only the people who love you? Even the tax collectors do that! And if you speak only to your friends, have you done anything out of the ordinary? Even the pagans do that! You must be perfect—just as your Father in heaven is perfect.

—Matthew 5:43-48, TEV

THIS IS ONE OF THE CLEAREST and perhaps most demanding New Testament passages for interpreting the meaning of love.

We are commanded to love our enemies. Why? In order that we may be children of God—in order that we may be like God. And what is the action cited? God sends the rain on the just and the unjust. Don't miss this. No matter what we are like, God acts in love toward us. Love is the heartbeat of God.

Look at the man who wrote the great hymn of love—Paul himself. You know his story. We meet him in the Book of Acts as the fellow who was hell-bent on destroying this new movement—these followers of Christ. He went on a mission to Damascus to seek to stomp out the church, to put to death all those who, in his mind, were blaspheming God by claiming Christ as the Messiah. Now think about this—that such a man could be so transformed and inwardly renewed

that he could see, touch, and handle with such profound spiritual delicacy, the concept of the divine love in its very essence, offers the ultimate testimony of the miracle of grace to which he spent the rest of his life bearing witness. If we can follow St. Paul to the heights of his vision of the nature of love, we can draw as near to the heart of God as human beings ever can. Preacher, prophet, priest, and poet, those many parts of Paul, seem to unite to proclaim, once and for all, the nature of that love which is divine and which excels all human loves (Duncan, p. 1).

Ever since Paul, others have expressed that grace and have known that love is the heartbeat of God.

Not long ago I sat with a young woman to whom life had dealt a tragic blow. An uncaring husband had walked all over her—had trampled her feelings—her very heart—in the mud. She had given herself to him, and he had used her. It was a despicable kind of harshness on his part.

It would have been a normal thing for her to be calloused and hard. The pain was there and she wept a lot—but there was a tenderness about her, a kind of transparent perception of reality that defied reason, and she expressed it in a few words: "This is not the end for me—though I'm beaten down and crushed. This is not the end for me, because I know I am loved by God."

Reflecting and Recording

Spend some time thinking about love as the heartbeat of God. Recall scripture verses you have memorized that speak of God as love.

What about your favorite hymns, or hymns you may sing often? Think of the ones that name and affirm the love of God. Sing some of the words you know.

As an act of praise to the God of love, repeat aloud John 3:16:

For God so loved the world, that he gave his only begotten Son, that whosoever believeth in him should not perish, but have everlasting life.

—John 3:16, KJV

During the Day

If you do not know John 3:16 by heart, copy it on a piece of paper you can take with you. At every possible pause or break during the day, read this verse or repeat it from memory.

Day Seven

A CHRISTIAN: ONE WHO LOVES

I give you a new commandment, that you love one another.
Just as I have loved you, you also should love one another.

—John 13:34

Jesus did not just *commend* love as a noble way of life, he *commanded* it as the rule of the kingdom, the way we are to live as his disciples. Leonard Evans put it this way, "The Kingdom of God is where the love which the Father has for the Son has been implanted in our hearts through the Cross, imparted and invigorated by the Holy Spirit so that you and I can love one another like the Father loves the Son and the Son loves the Father" (Harper, p. 96).

After quoting Evans, Michael Harper writes,

Leonard Evans' definition, which helps us to see this flow of love within the Trinity, to the Church and to the world, is also a definition of the Kingdom. One does not normally associate the concept of the Kingdom with love. The words seem totally different, even antithetic. Kingdom suggests rule, authority and power. Whereas love suggests care and concern. Love is more gentle, even tender in its application. But on the contrary it would seem most important that the two words are closely and carefully related to each other. Like truth and righteousness the word kingdom is part of what love is all about. For the kingdom we should be concerned about is the Kingdom of God, and since God is love, presumably the Kingdom will be the Kingdom of his love. Victor Furnish puts this well, "The rule of God is the rule of love. Love is the law of life in the Kingdom . . . love is . . . the power and the purpose of God's coming and reign" (Harper, p. 97).

A Christian is one who loves, and life in the kingdom is a life of love—loving God and loving others.

It is instructive to remember that Jesus' word, "By this everyone will know that you are my disciples, if you have love for one another" (John 13:35) was spoken at the Last Supper after Jesus had washed the disciples' feet. And, it was just before the betrayal of Judas. These men were anything but loving. The Crucifixion and Resurrection of Jesus, his ascension into heaven, and the coming of the Holy Spirit at Pentecost radically changed them. Love grew until it became the distinguishing mark of Christianity in the first two centuries.

As already stated, God is love and Jesus is God's definition of love. In the New Testament love is always the revelation of God in Jesus Christ.

Reflecting and Recording

When we love as Jesus loved, we are living in the kingdom. Spend some time thinking about the fact that Jesus did not simply *commend* love, he *commanded* it.

Continue your reflection along these lines: If I respond to Jesus' command to love as a discipline, will there come a time when I will love spontaneously without having to remind myself, "this is my duty"?

During the Day

Keep note of occasions today when you love as a deliberate effort, because you are commanded, and when you love spontaneously, naturally.

GROUP MEETING FOR WEEK ONE

Introduction

These group sessions will be most meaningful as they reflect the experience of all the participants. This guide is simply an effort to facilitate personal sharing. Therefore, I encourage you not to be too rigid in following the suggestions below. The leader, especially, should seek to be sensitive to what is going on in the lives of the participants and to help focus the group's sharing on those experiences.

I want to call one other thing to the attention of the leaders. Ideas are important. We should wrestle with new ideas as well as with ideas with which we disagree. It is important, however, that the group meeting not become a debate about ideas. The emphasis should be on the persons in the group and their experiences, feelings, and meanings.

On any subject, and certainly on the subject of love, people will have different ideas and experiences. These ideas should be acknowledged, affirmed, and celebrated. The sooner and more freely each person shares personally, the more helpful you will all be to each other. As the group comes to the place where all members can share honestly and openly what they have experienced and what is happening in their lives, these weekly sharing sessions will become increasingly meaningful.

Sharing Together

1. Begin your sharing time by inviting each person in the group to share his or her most meaningful day with the workbook this week. The leader should share first. Tell why that particular day was so meaningful.
2. On Day Two you were asked to identify a person who was a living expression of love and what made him/her so. Invite two or three persons to share and tell about the persons they identified.
3. Spend five to ten minutes discussing Augustine's word on Day Three: "Where love is, what can be wanting? Where love is not, what can possibly be profitable?"
4. Invite two or three persons to share their experiences of love as "energized goodwill" (Day Four).
5. Spend five to ten minutes talking about the Cross and its meaning in your life. Press one another to be personal.
6. If you have any time left, talk about how far along we are in loving spontaneously, without having to remind ourselves that "love is my duty."

Praying Together

Each week the group is asked to pray together. Corporate prayer is one of the great blessings of Christian community. There is power in corporate prayer, and it is important that this dimension be included in our shared pilgrimage.

It is also important that you feel comfortable in this and that no pressure be placed on anyone to pray aloud. Silent corporate prayer may be as vital and meaningful as verbal corporate prayer. God does not need to hear our verbal words to hear our prayers. Silence, where thinking is centered and attention is focused, may provide our deepest periods of prayer.

There is power, however, whenever members of a community on a common journey verbalize their thoughts and feelings to God in the presence of each other. I would strongly suggest that verbal prayers be offered spontaneously as a person chooses to pray aloud—not "let's go around the circle now, and each one pray."

Other suggestions for this time of praying together will be given each week. The leader for the week should regard these only as suggestions. What is happening in the meeting—the mood, the needs that are expressed, the timing—should determine the direction of the group prayer. Here are some possibilities for this closing period.

1. Enter this closing prayer time by asking two or three volunteers to read or quote a verse or verses of scripture that speak of God as love.

2. Sing a hymn or song everyone might know about the love of God or Jesus, for example, "Jesus Loves Me."

3. Invite group members to spend time in silent prayer. Invite them to think about each person in the group and offer a one-sentence silent prayer for each person, basing their prayers on what that person may have shared in the meeting, or what they know otherwise about that person. (The leader should judge the time by his or her own practice of this exercise.)

4. Let the leader close with a verbal prayer or contact someone ahead of time to offer a closing prayer.

Picture Taking

Before everyone leaves, take a picture of each person in the group with an instant or Polaroid camera. Then turn the pictures face down on the table and let each person select and take one home. This is the person for whom you will pray specifically this week. Before you go, take a few minutes to visit with the person whose picture you chose, getting to know him or her better. Ask if there are things coming up in that person's life about which you might pray.

Bring the pictures back to the group meeting each week, shuffle them face down, and let each person select a new person for whom to pray during the following week.

Week Two

The Primacy of Love

JESUS' MESSAGE: LOVE

If I speak in the tongues of mortals and of angels, but do not have love, I am a noisy gong or a clanging cymbal. And if I have prophetic powers, and understand all mysteries and all knowledge, and if I have all faith, so as to remove mountains, but do not have love, I am nothing. If I give away all my possessions, and if I hand over my body so that I may boast, but do not have love, I gain nothing.

—1 Corinthians 13:1-3

FIRST CORINTHIANS 13 IS ONE OF THE MOST transparent expressions of truth in the Bible. To even comment on it is like "gilding the lily," or offering an explanation of Leonardo Da Vinci's *Mona Lisa* or Beethoven's *Fifth Symphony*. We want to live with it and experience it, not simply offer commentary.

We call this passage Paul's "hymn of love." Because it is a great piece of poetry, it is easy to read and to relish its beauty, and yet miss the radical and liberating truth of what Paul is saying.

Back in April of 1988, television cameras in Belfast, Ireland, recorded scenes of two British soldiers being beaten and fatally shot. It was one of the most terrible moments in that seemingly endless series of terrible moments as a people war with each other—covered by the misnamed mantel of "Protestant versus Roman Catholic." Those two soldiers happened down the wrong street at the wrong time. They died after being brutally beaten. It was all on videotape; and, thus, on the evening news around the world.

The Christian Science Monitor (April 1, 1988) recorded something that was not on the tape, and that did not make the evening news. This was the picture of a Roman Catholic woman—a member of that area's St.

Agnes Parish—who took her coat from around her shoulders and gently covered the nearly-naked body of one of the dead Protestant soldiers. She then bowed her head and prayed for him. Later her priest, the Reverend Tom Toler, said, "The only part the world tends to hear about Northern Ireland is the violence. But that woman was a typical St. Agnes parishioner." The newspaper continued, "These are not easy times for Father Toler and his flock. But then, preaching Jesus' word and following His example have never been easy—for Catholics or Protestants—in a province where politics and religion can be used as a double-edged sword."

We could recall any number of situations that witness to this same point: "Preaching Jesus' word and following his example has never been easy." At the heart of Jesus' word is love, and the Roman Catholic woman in Belfast knows it.

John captured this in his First Epistle:

> If we walk in the light as he himself is in the light, we have fellowship with one another, and the blood of Jesus his Son cleanses us from all sin. If we say that we have no sin, we deceive ourselves, and the truth is not in us. If we confess our sins, he who is faithful and just will forgive us our sins and cleanse us from all unrighteousness. If we say that we have not sinned, we make Him a liar, and His word is not in us.
>
> —1 John 1:7-10

Reflecting and Recording

Recall an experience when love made demands on you. Spend some time reflecting on what you learned from that experience.

During the Day

Look for "little ways" to express love today.

| Day Two |

FOUR KINDS OF LOVE

THE POWER AND BEAUTY OF 1 CORINTHIANS 13 is enhanced by different translations of scripture. You will see this in reading the first three verses from the New Revised Standard Version and Today's English Version.

New Revised Standard Version
If I speak in the tongues of mortals and of angels, but do not have love, I am a noisy gong or a clanging cymbal. And if I have prophetic powers, and understand all mysteries and all knowledge, and if I have all faith, so as to remove mountains, but do not have love, I am nothing. If I give away all my possessions, and if I hand over my body so that I may boast, but do not have love, I gain nothing.
—1 Corinthians 13:1-3

Today's English Version
I may be able to speak the languages of men and even of angels, but if I have no love, my speech is no more than a noisy gong or a clanging cymbal. I may have the gift of inspired preaching; I may have all knowledge and understand all secrets; I may have all the faith needed to move mountains—but if I have no love I am nothing. I may give away everything I have, and even give up my body to be burned—but if I have no love, this does me no good.
—1 Corinthians 13:1-3

You can't miss it, can you? No matter who I am, what I believe, who I know, or what I do—if I don't have love, I am nothing at all. Love is primary.

Let's underscore the primacy of love by looking at four kinds of love.

Greek is one of the richest of all languages, often having a whole series of words to express different shades of meaning in one conception, while English will have only one. In English, we have only one word to express many different kinds of love. Greek has no fewer than four.

There is the word *eros*, with its verb *eran*. These terms are mainly used to express love between the sexes. They can also be used for such things as the passion for ambition and the intensity of patriotism—but characteristically they are the words for physical love.

Then there is the word *storgē*, with its verb form *stergein*, which designates family affection. This noun and verb can be used to express the love of people within the context of the family—but also of a people for their ruler or their nation. For the most part, this expression is used to describe the love of parents for children and children for their parents.

The most common of all the Greek words for love is the noun *philia* and its verb form *philein*. This word has a lovely warmth about it. It means to look on someone with affectionate regard. It can be used for the love of friendship and the love of husband and wife. It's best translated "cherish" and it includes physical love, but a lot of other things as well. It can sometimes even mean "to kiss." In the New Testament, *philein* is used of the love of father and mother and son and daughter. We see it in Matthew 10:37: "Whoever loves father or mother more than me is not worthy of me; and whoever loves son or daughter more than me is not worthy of me."

It was used of the love of Jesus for Lazarus: "So the sisters sent a message to Jesus, 'Lord, he whom you love is ill'" (John 11:3). Once it was used of the love of Jesus for the beloved disciple, John: "So she ran and went to Simon Peter and the other disciple, the one whom Jesus loved, and said to them, 'They have taken the Lord out of the tomb and we do not know where they have laid him'" (John 20:2).

Philia and *philein* are beautiful words to express a beautiful relationship. (This word study is taken from *New Testament Words* by William Barclay.)

There is a fourth Greek expression for love, *agape*, which we will look at tomorrow.

Reflecting and Recording

By each of the Greek expressions of love, name and/or describe briefly your most recent experience of this kind of love.

Eros _____

_____

_____

Storgē _____

_____

_____

Philia _____

_____

_____

Reflect on the differences in these "loves." Which comes closest to your understanding of God's love?

During the Day

Pay attention to your relationships today, observing the different expressions of love.

| Day Three |

AGAPE

You have heard that it was said, 'You shall love your neighbor and hate your enemy.' But I say to you, Love your enemies and pray for those who persecute you, so that you may be children of your Father in heaven; for he makes his sun to rise on the evil and on the good, and sends rain on the righteous and on the unrighteous. For if you love those who love you, what reward do you have? Do not even the tax collectors do the same? And if you greet only your brothers and sisters, what more are you doing than others? Do not even the Gentiles do the same? Be perfect, therefore, as your heavenly Father is perfect.

—Matthew 5:43-48

BY FAR, THE MOST COMMON New Testament word for love is the noun *agape*, with its verb form *agapan*. This is a unique New Testament word. It is all-encompassing.

Agape is not a classical word at all; in fact it is doubtful if there is any classical instance of it. It has become the key word of the New Testament in expressing love and the ethics of a Christian.

Barclay reminds us that the great reason why Christian thought centered on *agape*, is that *agape* demands the exercise of the whole person. Christian love must not only extend to our nearest and our dearest—our friends and those who love us—Christian love must extend to the Christian fellowship, to the neighbor, to the enemy, to all the world. So Jesus said, "If you love those who love you, what reward have you? Do not even the tax collectors do the same?" (Matthew 5:46, NKJV)

Now, all the ordinary words for love are words which express an emotion. They are words which have to do with the heart. They express an experience which comes to us unsought, and, in a way, inevitably. We cannot help loving our kith and kin; blood is thicker than water. We speak about *falling in love*. That kind of love is not an achievement; it is something which happens to us and which we cannot help. There is no particular virtue in falling in love. It is something with which we have little or nothing consciously to do; it simply happens. But *agape* is far more than that.

Agape has to do with the *mind*: it is not simply an emotion which rises unbidden in our hearts; it is a principle by which we deliberately live. *Agape* has supremely to do with the *will*. It is a conquest, a victory, and achievement. No one ever naturally loved his enemies. To love one's enemies is a conquest of all our natural inclinations and emotions (Barclay, pp. 20-21).

This *agape*, this Christian love, is not merely a spontaneous emotional experience. It is the result of deliberate thought and action. It is, in fact, the act of loving the unlovable—loving people whom we do not like.

> Christianity does not ask us to love our enemies and to love men at large in the same way as we love our nearest and our dearest and those who are closest to us; that would be at one and the same time impossible and wrong. But it does demand that we should have at all times a certain attitude of the mind and a certain direction of the will towards all men, no matter who they are (Barclay, p. 21).

Reflecting and Recording

Someone has defined a real friend as "one who will stick by you when you come unglued." Another has given friendship this perspective: "A brother may not always be a friend, but a friend will always be a brother."

Who is one person among your relationships, apart from spouse, children, or parents, who loves you with an *agape* love? Name that person here.

Think about this person and offer a prayer of thanksgiving for what he or she has *been* and *done* for you.

During the Day

Practice identifying *agape* love as you express it or see it expressed today.

Day Four

JESUS AND *AGAPE*

ASK THE NEW TESTAMENT QUESTION, "What is love?" and the answer is clear: Jesus Christ. In his book *Ethics*, Dietrich Bonhoeffer spoke categorically:

> Only he who knows God knows what love is . . . love is the revelation of God . . . love has its origin not in us but in God . . . love is inseparably bound up with the name of Jesus Christ as the revelation of God. The New Testament answers the question "what is love?" quite unambiguously by pointing solely and entirely to Jesus Christ. He is the only definition of love . . . love is not what He *does* and what He *suffers*, but it is what *He* does and what *He* suffers. Love is always He Himself . . . love is always the revelation of God in Jesus Christ (Harper, p. 69).

The word was made flesh so that love might be seen, heard, and touched. How clearly Michael Harper makes this case:

> For just thirty-three years a small corner of the world saw perfect love manifested. That life was recorded faithfully by those who witnessed it. Wicked men tried to destroy that life. But Jesus Christ rose from the grave and in the Holy Spirit bequeathed that same life and love to all those who would believe and obey him. From the one epicenter of Bethlehem and Calvary a seismic shock wave of divine love has continuously shaken the world. That is what Christianity is about (Harper, p. 68).

In Jesus and thus in the New Testament and the Christian faith love is central. Not a saccharine, sentimental emotional response, not just warmth and good feelings, but *agape*. To be sure, aspects of *eros, storgē,* and *philia* may be encompassed in it. But when we talk of the love that defines the Christian we are talking about *agape*—a love that has no limits and makes no conditions. It is love "in Christ."

Reflecting and Recording

Take some time to reflect on Bonhoeffer's sentence, paying attention to the italic emphases: Jesus Christ "is the only definition of love . . . love is not what he *does* and what He *suffers*, but it is what *He* does and what *He* suffers. Love is always He Himself . . . love is always the revelation of God in Jesus Christ."

During the Day

Jesus defined love in his actions. Stay sensitive today to how your actions define love.

Day Five

CHRIST OR CUPID

Beloved, let us love one another, because love is from God; everyone who loves is born of God and knows God. Whoever does not love does not know God, for God is love. God's love was revealed among us in this way: God sent his only Son into the world so that we might live through him. In this is love, not that we loved God but that he loved us and sent his Son to be the atoning sacrifice for our sins. Beloved, since God loved us so much, we also ought to love one another. No one has ever seen God; if we love one another, God lives in us, and his love is perfected in us.

—1 John 4:7-12

No injunction is more fundamental to the message of scripture than those simple words of John, "let us love one another." The only way we know how to do this is to look and learn from Jesus.

A common symbol of love in our culture is Cupid. Is there any reader not familiar with this baby in a diaper with a bow and arrow? Once smitten by Cupid's arrow we are hopelessly "in love." More often than not, Cupid is not only portrayed with a bow and arrow, but is also blindfolded.

Many of us live as though love were that innocent (weak) and that naive (blind). How foreign this is to the love of God revealed in Jesus. As we know, Jesus' love took him to a cross. Hands extended in love always return covered with scars if not nailed to a cross.

Reflecting and Recording

Spend a minute or two pondering the assertion: "Hands extended in love always return covered with scars."

Recall your most recent experience when loving another cost you something—misunderstanding, rejection, verbal abuse, emotional pain. Make some notes here about that experience—when, where, who, why, circumstances, feelings as you recall them.

Where is the experience now? Has good come out of it? Is there still confusion and/or unresolved conflict? Is there some additional effort you need to put forth?

Pray about this situation and for the persons involved.

During the Day

As you move through the day, take note of expressions of Cupid-love and Christ-love.

Day Six

THE NEW COMMANDMENT FOR KEEPING
ALL THE OLD COMMANDMENTS

And now faith, hope, and love abide, these three; and the greatest of these is love.

—1 Corinthians 13:13

THIS IS PAUL'S CONCLUSION to his "hymn of love."

The most famous book written about this passage is Henry Drummond's *The Greatest Thing in the World*. The book began as an impromptu exposition. It took place on the lawn of a garden in Kent, England. The evangelist Dwight L. Moody was so exhausted after much preaching and speaking that he was not able to address the guests who had gathered to hear him in a garden at the home of a friend. He called his young friend and colleague, Henry Drummond, to undertake the task for him. So, in a spontaneous, impromptu sort of way, the little book, *The Greatest Thing in the World*, was born—a spiritual classic that will endure for all time.

In this masterpiece, Drummond reminds us that Paul said, "Love is the fulfilling of the law." Did you ever wonder what Paul meant by that?

In those days men were working their passage to Heaven by keeping the Ten Commandments, and the hundred and ten other commandments which they had manufactured out of them. Christ said, I will show you a more simple way. If you do one thing, you will do these hundred and ten things, without ever thinking about them. If you love, you will unconsciously fulfil the whole law. And you can readily see for yourselves how that must be so. Take any of the commandments. "Thou shalt have no other gods before Me." If a man love God, you will not require to tell him that. Love is the fulfilling of that law. "Take not His name in vain." Would he ever dream of taking His name in vain if he loved Him? "Remember the Sabbath day to keep it holy." Would he not be too glad to have one day in seven to dedicate more exclusively to the object of his affection? . . . In this way "Love is the fulfilling of the law." It is the rule for fulfilling all rules, the new commandment for keeping all the old commandments, Christ's one secret of the Christian life.

Urban T. Holmes III has coined the word, *mystogogue*. It defines the Christian who seeks to understand the encounter between the human and the sacred, and how that encounter transforms life into religious vocation. Paul became a mystagogue on the Damascus road. His vocation changed from revolutionary hatred to revolutionary love. He described the dramatic result of his encounter with the incarnation of love in Jesus Christ in these words:

> For the love of Christ urges us on, because we are convinced that one has died for all; therefore all have died. And he died for all, so that those who live might live no longer for themselves, but for him who died and was raised for them.
>
> From now on, therefore, we regard no one from a human point of view, even though we once knew Christ from a human point of view, we know him no longer in that way. So if anyone is in Christ, there is a new creation: everything old has passed away; see, everything has become new! All this is from God, who reconciled us to himself through Christ, and has given us the ministry of reconciliation; that is, in Christ, God was reconciling the world to himself, not counting their trespasses against them, and entrusting the message of reconciliation to us.
>
> —2 Corinthians 5:14-19

The new commandment, love, keeps all the old commandments and creates a new person.

Reflecting and Recording

Recall the last conversation you had with someone about love. Next to the listed categories below, make notes about the conversation:

Love of God

Love of Christ

Love between humans

In the conversation, how much was said about the commandments? the Law? Was anything said about being able to "do right" because of love?

During the Day

In your activity and relationships today, check whether your "doing right" is the result of law or love.

Day Seven

"GUERRILLA GOODNESS"

AMONG MY MYRIAD COLLECTION OF COFFEE MUGS, one has this inscription: "Practice random kindness and senseless acts of beauty." This slogan has appeared in all sorts of places; however, few know its origin. It just appeared, and a kind of movement has been motivated by it.

A woman visiting a friend noticed a card on her friend's refrigerator that said, "Practice random kindness and senseless acts of beauty." The next day she tried it. She was going across the Bay Bridge from Sausalito to San Francisco. She gave the man in the toll booth seven commuter tickets and said, "this is for me and for the next six people in line behind me." One after another, the cars approached the toll booth, hands reaching out the windows with dollar bills to pay the toll. The toll collector just waved the drivers on across the bridge, saying, "It's been taken care of. Have a nice day." I'm sure these persons did, and I also imagine that the people they worked with had a nice day as well.

The message once appeared as graffiti on a wall. Another woman saw it, wrote it down, and gave it to her husband, who is a seventh grade teacher. He put it on the chalkboard in his classroom. One of his students copied it down and showed it to her mother, who is a newspaper columnist. This mother wrote about it in the newspaper, asking, "Where did this come from?"

Two days later she heard from Anne Herbert of Marin County, whose original idea it was. Anne had thought of it while sitting in a Sausalito restaurant, and wrote it down on a paper placemat. The man next to her saw it, copied it down, and that's how it got started. Now it's spreading. It's on bumper stickers, business cards, in articles, and is spreading by word of mouth; and now I've told you about it. "Practice random kindness and senseless acts of beauty."

Mark Trotter, who traced the movement of the message, said,

the article that I read called this "guerrilla goodness." Not the animal in the rain forest, not the "gorilla of my dreams," but the French word which means "little war." Those who fight behind the lines in occupied territories. Guerrilla fighters are those who believe so strongly in what they are doing that they keep on fighting when everyone else has surrendered. They keep going, performing acts of subversion, because they believe these random acts will make a difference some day. Maybe not immediately, and maybe not in any calculable or measurable way, but cumulatively. These random acts wear down the enemy until that time when other people gain the courage to join in the struggle (Trotter, February 23, 1992).

This is the message of Jesus to us:

But I say to you that listen, Love your enemies, do good to those who hate you, bless those who curse you, pray for those who abuse you. If anyone strikes you on the cheek, offer the other also; and from anyone who takes away your coat do not withhold even your shirt. Give to everyone who begs from you; and if anyone takes away your goods, do not ask for them again. Do to others as you would have them do to you.

If you love those who love you, what credit is that to you? For even sinners love those who love them. If you do good to those who do good to you, what credit is that to you? For even sinners do the same. If you lend to those from whom you hope to receive, what credit is that to you? Even sinners lend to sinners, to receive as much again. But love your enemies, do good, and lend, expecting nothing in return. Your reward will be great, and you will be children of the Most High; for he is kind to the ungrateful and the wicked. Be merciful, just as your Father is merciful.

—Luke 6:27-36

Jesus is calling for "guerrilla goodness"—*agape* love.

Reflecting and Recording

Read again the above scripture. Consider it as a description of the way Christians are to behave in the world. Ponder your own patterns of relating and acting. Write a prayer, confessing your failure to live according to Jesus' call.

During the Day

This day and the days ahead seek to "practice random kindness and senseless acts of beauty."

GROUP MEETING FOR WEEK TWO

Introduction

Participation in a group such as this is a covenant relationship. You will profit the most as you keep the daily discipline of the thirty-minute period and as you faithfully attend these weekly meetings. Do not feel guilty if you have to miss a day in the workbook or if you are not able to give the full thirty minutes in daily disciplines. Don't hesitate sharing this with the group. We may learn something about ourselves as we share. We may discover, for instance, that we are unconsciously afraid of dealing with the content of a particular day because of what is required and what it reveals about us. Be patient with yourself and always be open to what God may be seeking to teach you.

Our growth, in part, hinges upon our group participation, so share as openly and honestly as you can. Listen to what persons are saying. Sometimes there is meaning beyond the surface of their words that you may pick up if you are really attentive.

To be a sensitive participant in this fashion is crucial. To respond immediately to the feelings we pick up is also crucial. Sometimes it is important for the group to focus its entire attention upon a particular individual. If some need or concern is expressed, it may be appropriate for the leader to ask the group to enter into a brief period of special prayer for the persons or concerns revealed. Participants should not always depend upon the leader for this kind of sensitivity, as the leader may miss it. Even if you aren't the leader, do not hesitate to ask the group to join you in special prayer. This may be silent prayer, or some person may wish to lead the group in prayer.

Remember, you have a contribution to make to the group. What you consider trivial or unimportant may be just what another person needs to hear. We are not seeking to be profound, but simply to share our experience.

Sharing Together

NOTE: It may not be possible in this time frame to use all these suggestions. The leader should select what will be most beneficial to the group. It is important that the leader be thoroughly familiar with these suggestions in order to move through them selectively according to the direction in which the group is moving and according to the time available. The leader should plan ahead, but do not hesitate to change your plan according to the nature of the sharing that takes place and the needs that emerge.

1. Open your time together with the leader offering a brief prayer of thanksgiving for the opportunity of sharing with the group and of petition for openness and love in sharing and responding to each other.
2. Let each person share his or her most meaningful day in this week's workbook adventure.
3. Now share the most difficult day and tell why it was difficult.
4. Invite two to three volunteers to share an experience when love made demands of them and what they learned from that experience.
5. Spend ten to fifteen minutes discussing the different expressions of love: *eros, storgē,* and *philia.* Use the experiences of these kinds of love which you identified on Day Two to make the discussion personal.
6. Spend five to ten minutes discussing the uniqueness of *agape* love, especially with reference to Jesus' revelation of *agape.*
7. Invite one or two volunteers to share an experience of love that cost something, and what has come from that experience.
8. Spend the time you have left talking about how we might spread "guerrilla goodness" (Day Seven).

Praying Together

As stated last week, the effectiveness of this group and the quality of relationship will be enhanced by a commitment to pray for each other by name each day. If you have the pictures of each person, as requested last week, put these pictures face-down on a table and let each person select a picture. This person will be the focus of special prayer for the week. Bring the photos back next week, shuffle them, and draw again. Continue this throughout your group life together. Looking at a person's picture as you pray for that person will add meaning. Having the picture will also remind you that you are to give special prayer attention to this person during the week.

1. To pray corporately each week is a special ministry. Take some time now for a period of verbal prayer, allowing each person to mention any special needs he or she wishes to share with the

entire group. Some persons might want to share the confusion or unresolved conflict they identified on Day Five that is the result of seeking to love at some cost.

2. Close your time by praying the great prayer of the church, the Lord's Prayer. As you pray this prayer, remember that you are linking yourselves with all Christians of all time in universal intercession.

3. Make sure each person gets a new picture of a person for prayer this week.

Words of Encouragement

Here are some of my thoughts as you begin the third week of this journey:

1. Discipline is an important dimension of life. Discipline is not slavish rigidity, but an ordering of life that enables you to control your circumstances rather than to be controlled by them. For most people, a designated time of prayer is essential for building a life of prayer.

2. If you have not yet established a regular time for both prayer and to use this workbook, try to find the right time for you this week. Experiment with the morning, after work, during lunch hour, or before retiring. Find the time that seems best for you.

3. If you discover that you can't cover all the workbook material and exercises given for a day, do not berate yourself. Get what you can out of what you do. There is no point in rushing over three or four steps or principles if you cannot think deeply. Consider each step seriously, one by one, and move only as far as you can.

4. Intellectual assent to a great principle or possibility is important, but it does us little good until we act upon it—until we say yes in our minds, and live it out in relationships.

5. Don't hesitate to make decisions and resolutions, but do not condemn yourself if you fail. God is patient, and God wants us to be patient with ourselves.

WEEK THREE

If I
Have
Not
Love

IF I HAVE NOT LOVE, I AM NOTHING

If I speak in the tongues of mortals and of angels, but do not have love, I am a noisy gong or a clanging cymbal. And if I have prophetic powers, and understand all mysteries and all knowledge, and if I have all faith, so as to remove mountains, but do not have love, I am nothing. If I give away all my possessions, and if I hand over my body so that I may boast, but do not have love, I gain nothing.

Love is patient; love is kind; love is not envious or boastful or arrogant or rude. It does not insist on its own way; it is not irritable or resentful; it does not rejoice in wrongdoing, but rejoices in the truth. It bears all things, believes all things, hopes all things, endures all things.

—1 Corinthians 13:1-7

THOMAS S. KEPLER WAS A NEW TESTAMENT PROFESSOR at Oberlin College in Ohio. He was a gifted writer, scholar, and teacher. It was through his book, *Journey with the Saints*, that I was introduced to the richness of spiritual biography and the resources for spiritual formation in the "cloud of witnesses" sense of New Testament days—a cloud of witnesses who have demonstrated the Christian way for us.

Through most of his teaching career he was also pastor of a little rural church in northern Medina County in Ohio. Midway through his teaching career, his brothers and sisters of the seminary faculty noticed a change in his life. As someone said, "the Christian graces of life—'the fruit of the Spirit'—settled comfortably upon him."

This change was never understood until the time of his death. His wife then found a little piece of paper in the back of his wallet. It was folded into a small square. On the paper he had written a date and these words: "This is the moment of rededication to Jesus Christ as my Lord and Savior. This moment is private. The fruit of this moment will be known only as others see Christ reflected in me." It was signed with the date and time, and with the words, "Your Servant, Tom Kepler."

The "fruit of the Spirit" was known in Thomas Kepler. Paul is telling us in the first verses of his hymn of love that if the fruit of Christ's grace in us—love—is not known, we are nothing.

Here is the phrase I want us to spend our time thinking about this week. This one phrase: "But have not love" (KJV).

It occurs three times in the first three verses (in slightly different wording in other translations).

"If I speak in the tongues of mortals and angels, but do not have love . . ."

"If I have prophetic powers, and understand all mysteries and all knowledge, and if I have all faith, so as to remove mountains, but do not have love . . ."

"If I give away all my possessions, and if I hand over my body so that I may boast, but do not have love . . ."

Paul makes his point clearly. He speaks radically, and we don't miss what he is saying. Nothing is of any use if love is missing.

Back in 1991, a news reporter asked Al Davis, co-owner and general manager of the Los Angeles Raiders football team, which one of the following was most important to him: money, power, or love? Davis responded that the most important of the three was power. Why? Because if you have power then you can make money and secure love.

Paul would not agree with Mr. Davis; would you?

Reflecting and Recording

Name three or four of your most treasured *material possessions*.

1. _____

2. _____

3. _____

4. _____

What would happen to you if you lost these treasured material possessions? Think about it for two or three minutes. How would you feel? What would you do?

♥

Name three or four of your most *precious relationships*.

1. _____

2. _____

3. _____

4. _____

Now think about what would happen if you lost your most precious relationships. How would you feel? What would you do? Spend a few minutes reflecting on such a loss.

♥

Move now to another category. Name your two most outstanding talents or gifts (i.e., music, art, an ability to communicate, friendliness, the capacity to persevere).

1. _____

2. _____

What would happen if you lost these talents/gifts? How would you feel? What would you do? Spend a minute or two in reflection.

♥

Now think about this reflection experience in light of Paul's word: "If I do not have love, I am nothing."

♥

During the Day

First Corinthians 13:1-3 is printed on page 159. Cut it out, take it with you in the days ahead—in your pocket, purse, or wallet. Take it out as often as possible, read it prayerfully, and begin to memorize it.

Day Two

IF I DO NOT HAVE LOVE, I BECOME LESS THAN HUMAN

PAUL SAYS, IF I DO NOT HAVE LOVE, I AM NOTHING. He is talking about being a loving person. It doesn't matter whether I'm rich, or richly gifted with talent, or highly successful, or in a place of prestige and power. Even with all that, if I am not loving, then I am nothing. This is the primary point Paul is making.

Let's look at this haunting phrase, "if I do not have love, I am nothing," from another perspective.

If I do not have love, I become less than human.

Here is a picture of this. I was preaching at a laity conference in North Carolina. Over two thousand people were present, and they were a great audience. After my first sermon, people stood in a line to greet me.

I saw a woman sort of hang back. She wanted a bit more time than the usual greeting and "thank you" that are the normal exchanges with a preacher after the sermon. I gave this to her. She was not from North Carolina. She had used a number of my workbooks with groups in her church. She wanted this opportunity to meet and hear me and had driven five hundred miles to attend the conference. I was moved by her affirmation and the fact that she would drive that distance, especially at her age. She must have been about seventy years old. I was so touched by her extravagant expression of appreciation that I gave her a great big bear hug. You would have thought I had given a glass of water to a person dying of thirst, or one thousand dollars to a penniless beggar. Her face was aglow. "Thank you!" she said. And I know she didn't plan it, but spontaneously she added: "Nobody hugs me anymore."

She told me more about herself. She had lost her husband ten years before. Her children were scattered, she lived alone, and she didn't get hugs anymore.

Hugs and love go together. If I don't get hugged—if I don't get love—I become less than human.

Since hugging is a very good expression of love, let's take a little side trip in our reflection. Back in 1984, Kathleen Keating wrote a book called *The Hug Therapy Book*. In this book she contends that:

Hugs are not only nice; they are needed. They make you happier and healthier. . . . They help us overcome our fears and tensions and they even give you good, enjoyable exercise, especially if you hug energetically. . . .

There is the **A-frame hug** where you touch at the top . . . Good for an old great-aunt, or the boss's wife, or your teacher at the school.

There is the **back-to-front hug** . . . where the hugger wraps his/her arms around the huggee from the rear. Good for those peeling potatoes, scrubbing pans, picking raspberries, or sorting mail.

And, there is the **Heart to Heart Hug**, firm and gentle with heart, as it were, touching hearts—where real love comes from. A good bear hug can help you to bear anything.

That's true, because hugs are expressions of love. If I don't get hugged—that is, if I don't have love—I become less than human.

Reflecting and Recording

Has there been a time in your life when you did not feel loved? Make enough notes to recall that experience and describe your feelings.

If you are not still living in that state of feeling unloved, describe what happened to change it.

If you have always felt loved, spend some time thanking God for those who have loved you.

During the Day

Look for as many opportunities as possible to hug other people today. You never know how desperately they may need it.

Day Three

DON'T FORGET TO TOUCH AND HUG

Little children, let us love, not in word or speech, but in truth and action.

—1 John 3:18

THOUGH HE USES THE TERM "LITTLE CHILDREN," John is talking to all of us. He is calling us to love not just in word but in deed. We are to *show* our love.

Yesterday we considered the proposition that if we do not have love we become less than human. Let us now focus this in a special way.

As we grow older, we tend to grow careless of the ones we are supposed to love. We become thoughtless of the little things that keep love alive. So we don't hug as much as we should. We don't speak kind and loving words to our spouses. We take each other for granted—and to take another for granted is to make them less than human.

Words and actions can wound us, but so can the absence of words and actions. Indifference, disregard, neglect—those are painful bullets that can penetrate our hearts and bring emotional death. These deaths may be silent—we often don't see them happening, though people are dying right before our eyes. We don't see them because we are not looking and we are not listening. The ears and eyes of our hearts are closed to those around us—sometimes even to those we love.

Reflecting and Recording

On Day One you were asked to name your three or four most precious relationships. Go back to that list. Look at each one, asking yourself: Do I regularly express my love to this person—in word and deed?

During the Day

Write a letter to each of your "most precious relationships," or call them on the phone, telling them you love them.

Day Four

ONLY GRANDMA IS HERE!

Honor your father and your mother, so that your days may be long in the land that the Lord your God is giving you.

—Exodus 20:12

Listen to your father who begot you, and do not despise your mother when she is old.

—Proverbs 23:22

THE CALL TO HONOR OUR FATHERS AND MOTHERS is one of God's Ten Commandments, and the wisdom of such honor is underscored by the writer of Proverbs. If any particular group is threatened by the inhumanity of lack of love, it is the elderly, especially those who are in nursing homes.

When I was editor of *The Upper Room*, I met a struggling young writer, Donna Swanson. She had written one of the most poignant prose poems I have ever read. We published it first in *alive now!* It was later included in a collection of writings by women, entitled *Images*. Finally, a beautiful and powerful little four-minute movie was made of it.

This poem is one of the most gripping expressions I know of how the lack of love takes our life away and makes us less than human. It is entitled "Minnie Remembers."

God,
My hands are old.
I've never said that out loud before
but they are.
I was so proud of them once.
They were soft
like the velvet smoothness of a firm, ripe
peach.
Now the softness is more like worn-out sheets
or withered leaves.
When did these slender, graceful hands
become gnarled, shrunken claws?
When, God?
They lie here in my lap,
naked reminders of this worn-out
body that has served me too well!

How long has it been since someone touched me?
Twenty years?
Twenty years I've been a widow.
Respected.
Smiled at.
But never touched.
Never held so close that loneliness
was blotted out.

I remember how my mother used to hold me,
God.
When I was hurt in spirit or flesh,
she would gather me close,
stroke my silky hair
and caress my back with her warm hands.
O God, I'm so lonely!

I remember the first boy who ever kissed me.
We were both so new at that!
The taste of young lips and popcorn
the feeling inside of mysteries to come.

I remember Hank and the babies.
How else can I remember them but together?
Out of the fumbling, awkward attempts of new
lovers came the babies.
And as they grew, so did our love.
And, God, Hank didn't seem to mind
if my body thickened and faded a little.
He still loved it. And touched it.
And we didn't mind if we were no longer beautiful.
And the children hugged me a lot.
O God, I'm lonely!

God, why didn't we raise the kids to be silly
and affectionate as well as
dignified and proper?
You see, they do their duty.
They drive up in their fine cars;
they come to my room to pay their respects.
They chatter brightly, and reminisce.
But they don't touch me.
They call me "Mom" or "Mother"
or "Grandma."

Never Minnie.
My mother called me Minnie.
So did my friends.
Hank called me Minnie, too.
But they're gone.
And so is Minnie.
Only Grandma is here.
And God! She's lonely!

Those who are growing old—parents and loved ones, especially those living alone or in nursing homes—need to be loved. They need us to express our love *physically*.

Reflecting and Recording

Spend three or four minutes reflecting on "Minnie Remembers." Try to feel with Minnie. Also, question yourself about the Minnies in your life. You may want to read Minnie's prayer again.

During the Day

If you have a loved one or a friend in a nursing home or hospital, visit, call, or write to him or her today.

Day Five

IF WE DO NOT HAVE LOVE, WE DIE

For this is the message you have heard from the beginning, that we should love one another. We must not be like Cain who was from the evil one and murdered his brother. And why did he murder him? Because his own deeds were evil and his brother's righteous. Do not be astonished, brothers and sisters, that the world hates you. We know that we have passed from death to life because we love one another. Whoever does not love abides in death.

—1 John 3: 11-14

JOHN SPEAKS A STRONG WORD: "Whoever does not love abides in death" (1 John 3:14).

Paul uses the haunting phrase over and over again: "If I do not have love." In the past few days we have talked about the lack of love making us less than human. More extreme than that, if we do not have love, we die.

Dr. James J. Lynch wrote a book entitled *The Broken Heart: The Consequences of Loneliness*. In that book he made the point that

whether it be heart disease, cancer, alcoholism, accidents, disease or suicide, the mortality rate for those who [live] alone [is] from two to five times greater than those who [do] not. Social isolation and deprivation of meaningful human contacts seem to lead to organic difficulties, and even to death. The divorced, the widowed, and the otherwise unattached [have] by far the greatest problems.

When we are not loved, we lose the will to live. Poets know this—and so should we. Loneliness can kill us. W. H. Auden said, "We must love one another, or die." Loneliness can kill us—I mean *kill* us.

Now I know this is not precisely what Paul means when he says, "If I do not have love, I am nothing." But what he says suggests this. The haunting phrase, "but do not have love," drives the point home. "If I do not have love, I die."

A United Methodist pastor tells about the most passionate person he had ever known—a lady named Gladys. She was a retired school teacher who lived with her only child, a daughter, in the community where the pastor served his first church. Gladys loved everybody, and everybody loved her. When a new baby arrived, so did a homemade doll from Gladys. When a person went into the hospital, they soon received a card that Gladys was praying for them. At seventy years of age, she visited the old folks every week, and she inspired all the young folks as she did. When you were under the weather, homemade chicken soup from Gladys's kitchen was the medicine that always worked. Everybody in Franklin County, Kentucky, loved Gladys (except the chickens!).

One day something happened. Gladys had a terrible confrontation with her daughter. The younger woman packed up and moved out. Gladys was never the same. She sent no more notes to the living, and no more flowers to the dead. She made no more visits to neighbors, nor did she invite any of the neighbors into her home. Evidently she had been so hurt by her daughter that she made certain she would never be hurt again. She ended all relationships and acted as if she were the only person in the world.

But it didn't work. No matter what she tried, it did not work. Within six months, Gladys was dead.

Hers was the most painful death this young pastor had ever witnessed. There was no malignancy, and there was no physical torture. But the emotional pain was literally unbelievable. Gladys learned firsthand that even more painful than loving is the pain—the death—of not loving at all.

Reflecting and Recording
Go back to the beginning of today's session and read 1 John 3:11-14.

Spend a few minutes reflecting on this passage. Focus on the sentence, "Whoever does not love abides in death."

We can often become more centered in our prayer by writing our prayers. I call this "praying at the point of a pencil." It helps us to be clear, precise, and focused. Out of your reflection on the 1 John passage, write a prayer expressing your past experience in loving or failing to love, and your present feelings.

During the Day

Frank Laubach has taught us about "flash prayers": when we are waiting to cross the street or standing in a grocery line, when we hear a siren or are waiting for a traffic light to change; we can offer flash prayers—thank-yous or petitions to God.

We can also use such occasions for "flash scripture" reminders. Today, use the times you might use for flash prayers to call this word to mind: "Whoever does not love abides in death."

Day Six

HUG WITHDRAWAL

IN A "BEARS IN LOVE" CARTOON, ONE BEAR SAYS: "Here I sit all alone, because of a dumb fight with Trudy."

In the second frame he continues, "I could be hugging her, but instead I'm all alone." In the third frame, he concludes, "I think I'll go apologize before I start to go into hug withdrawal."

I hope that you do not see this as a superficial image: *hug withdrawal.* There are thousands of people around us who have gone into hug withdrawal. They have no one to hug them, to touch them, to love them. They are out of the mainstream, and over an extended period of time many will lose sight of their own humanity. If they are not given attention and love, they will turn against society, believing that society has turned against them.

Jesus began his public ministry quoting from Isaiah 61:

The Spirit of the Lord is upon me, because he has anointed me to bring good news to the poor. He has sent me to proclaim release to the captives and recovery of sight to the blind, to let the oppressed go free, to proclaim the year of the Lord's favor.

—Luke 4:18-19

After this reading, Jesus startled his synagogue congregation with his claim, "Today this scripture has been fulfilled in your hearing" (Luke 4:21). Some people believe this was merely the assigned reading for worship that day, but I don't. Jesus deliberately chose this text to announce his mission and ministry. This was to be his "Messianic platform" for the next three years.

The poor, not the rich; the weak, rather than the powerful; the no-name, no-place-in-the-sun people would receive his attention. This doesn't mean that Jesus loves only the weak, the poor, and the disenfranchised. It does mean that the closer we get to Jesus, the closer we will get to the people he loved.

It should be obvious that not only people who are out of the so-called mainstream feel marginalized. There are people who "have it made" by all material standards, but who are starved for love and authentic relationships. They need the warm affirmation of human attention and love. They need to know that Jesus loves them and so do we.

If we do not have love, we die.

Reflecting and Recording

Poet George Santa has written of the "men" (this includes all humankind) who walk the streets of our cities. Then he offers the response of the compassionate Christ.

We are the men of the city street,
We are the men whose footsteps beat
Weary marches through empty years
Dreary tempos to falling tears,
Men whose souls are damned by sin,
Men whose hearts are dead within,
Broken bodies—we dream of death
And joy in Life's receding breath. . . .
Broken souls, and the yawning grave
Holds more terrors than e'er it gave
Of respite to our motley lot;
We are the men that Life forgot.

I am the Christ of the city street,
I walk its miles with bleeding feet,

I see the men whose lives are spent
In deepest night and banishment
From all that human hearts hold dear,
I see the ghosts of men walk here.
I see their faces gaunt and thin,
The sinful hearts I long to win,
I know their burdens, feel their pain,
And yearn to turn their loss to gain;
I note the falter in their tread,
I see the pallor of the dead
Upon their faces, and I stand
To offer them My nail-scarred hand,
But now I weep, for even they
Sneer mockingly and turn away. . . .
Yes, of this city I'm a part—
I walk its streets with bleeding heart.
                              (Flynn, 11-12)

Reflect and pray in response to this poem.

Read again Jesus' announcement of his mission printed above.

During the Day

There are some passages of scripture that every Christian should memorize. I believe Luke 4:18-19 is one of these. You will find it printed on page 159. Cut it out and take it with you, along with 1 Corinthians 13:1-3—which hopefully you are already commiting to memory—for the next few days, taking opportune occasions to read these passages and commit them to memory.

Day Seven

IF I HAVE NOT LOVE

If I speak in the tongues of mortals and of angels, but do not have love, I am a noisy gong or a clanging cymbal. And if I have prophetic powers, and understand all mysteries and all knowledge, and if I have all faith, so as to remove mountains, but do not have love, I am nothing. If I give away all my possessions, and if I hand over my body so that I may boast but do not have love, I gain nothing.

—1 Corinthians 13:1-3

NOTHING IS OF ANY USE IF WE DON'T LOVE.

Go back to the story I shared on Day Five about Gladys, who was a love-giver until she and her daughter were estranged. Without her daughter's love, Gladys closed off relationships and soon died.

The man who told that story was the pastor of a large church. He had risen to the pinnacle of success—senior minister of this huge church before he was forty, known nationally for his gifts as a preacher, recognized with honors for his leadership.

Then came a shocking event. Someone attempted to kill his wife, and the police insisted he was the prime suspect. He was arrested, went to trial, and was acquitted—his wife still in a coma. Shortly after the attempted murder, he left town with his therapist, forsaking his comatose wife and leaving his two children in the care of friends.

This pastor had once said of Gladys, that member of his first congregation: "Hers was the most painful death I ever witnessed. There was no malignancy and there was no physical torture—but the emotional pain was literally unbelievable. Gladys learned firsthand that even more painful than loving is the pain of not loving at all."

This able pastor has proven Paul right: "Though I speak with the tongues of men and angels, and do not have love, I am a noisy gong and a clanging cymbal." Nothing is of any use without love.

Reflecting and Recording

In your reflecting and recording on Day One of this week, you were asked to name three or four relationships most precious to you. Go back to your list on page 58. Did you name Christ among those relationships?

Don't be embarrassed if you didn't. You may have thought only in terms of human relations. But think about it now.

Jesus himself said, "Abide in me as I abide in you. . . . as the Father has loved me, so I have loved you; abide in my love" (John 15: 4, 9). And John said, "Whoever does not love abides in death" (1 John 3:14).

Spend some time reflecting on the image of abiding in Christ as a way to abide in love. How does this enable us to escape death?

During the Day

Continue "living with" Jesus' announcement of his mission (Luke 4:18-19) until you memorize it.

If you are sharing this workbook journey with a group, read the instruction for the weekly gathering and prepare for the meeting.

GROUP MEETING FOR WEEK THREE

Introduction

Two essential ingredients of Christian fellowship are *feedback* and *follow-up*. Feedback is necessary to keep the group dynamic working positively for all participants. Follow-up is essential to express Christian concern and ministry.

The leader is primarily responsible for feedback in the group. All persons should be encouraged to share their feelings about how the group is functioning.

Listening is crucial. To listen to another, we are saying, "You are important; I value you." It is also crucial to check out meaning, in order that those who are sharing this pilgrimage with us can know that we are really listening to and hearing them. We so often *mis*-hear. "Are you saying _____?" is a good check question. It takes only a couple of persons in a group, who listen and give feedback in this fashion, to set the mood for the group.

Follow-up is the function of everyone. If we listen to what others are saying, we will discover needs and concerns beneath the surface, situations that deserve special prayer and attention. Make notes of these as the group shares. Follow up during the week with a telephone call, a written note of caring and encouragement, or a visit. What distinguishes a Christian fellowship is *caring in action* ("My, how those Christians love one another!"). Be sure to follow up each week with others in the group.

Sharing Together

By this time, a significant amount of "knowing" exists in the group. Group participants are feeling safe in the group, perhaps more willing to share. Still, there is no place for pressure. The leader, however, should be especially sensitive to those slow to share. Seek gently to coax them out. Every person is a gift to the group, and the gift is fully revealed by sharing. Be sure to save at least ten minutes for prayer at the close of this session.

1. Invite two volunteers to share their response to the loss of treasured *material possessions* as named and reflected upon on Day One.
2. Invite two volunteers to share their response to the loss of their most *precious relationships* as named and responded to on Day One.
3. Invite two persons to share their response to the loss of *talents/ gifts* as named and responded to on Day One.
4. Spend five to ten minutes discussing the importance of physical expressions of love, such as touching, hugging, and verbal expression.
5. Ask at least one volunteer to share an experience when he or she did not feel loved, and how that has changed, if it has.
6. Spend about ten minutes allowing persons to share their response to "Minnie Remembers" (Day Five).

Praying Together

1. The leader should take up the Polaroid pictures of the group, shuffle them, and let each person draw a new one.
2. Invite each member of the group to spend two minutes in quiet prayer for the person whose picture he or she has drawn, focusing on what that person has shared in this meeting.

3. Invite a couple of volunteers to share the prayers they wrote in their time of reflecting and recording on Day Five.

4. Close the time with sentence prayers, praying specifically about the needs shared by persons.

WEEK FOUR

Assessing
Our
Love
Life

THE MESSAGE WE HAVE HEARD FROM THE BEGINNING

Little children, let us love, not in word or speech, but in truth and action. And by this we will know that we are from the truth and will reassure our hearts before him whenever our hearts condemn us; for God is greater than our hearts, and he knows everything. Beloved, if our hearts do not condemn us, we have boldness before God, and we receive from him whatever we ask, because we obey his commandments and do what pleases him.

And this is his commandment, that we should believe in the name of his Son Jesus Christ and love one another, just as he has commanded us. All who obey his commandments abide in him, and he abides in them, by the Spirit that he has given us.

—1 John 3:18-24

THE SECTION OF SCRIPTURE IN WHICH THIS PASSAGE is found begins with the statement, "For this is the message you have heard from the beginning, that we should love one another" (1 John 3:11). This is a central message of the gospel, and certainly a primary call of Jesus.

A tramp one day knocked at the door of a Catholic rectory. "Father," he said to the priest, "I've been floating around for a long time, and I was wondering if I could join your church and settle down?"

"Why yes," said the priest, "I'd be happy for you to do that, but first let's find out what you know about faith."

With Christmas coming, he decided to ask the tramp a simple and seasonal question. "Where was Jesus born?" asked the priest.

Without even hesitating, the tramp said, "In Pittsburgh."

"No," said the priest, "I'm sorry, but it was not in Pittsburgh. Try again."

"O.K. . . . if he wasn't born in Pittsburgh, it must have been in Philadelphia." And again, the priest shook his head and said, "No, I'm sorry, that's not right."

But then, not wanting to embarrass the tramp any further, the priest decided to just tell him. Very slowly, he said, "Now get this: "Jesus was born in Bethlehem. Got it?"

And the tramp's face lit up. "Yeah . . . that's right . . . I just knew it was somewhere in Pennsylvania!" (Neaves, April 30, 1989)

I don't know where the priest took it from there, but I have an idea he loved the tramp no less and expressed no exasperation or rudeness—because from the feel of the story, the priest was a person who loved the Jesus way, which is the theme of our workbook.

We probably know more about Jesus than the tramp did. But do we *know* the message heard from the beginning? We are to be loving.

A. J. Cronin was a Scottish doctor turned novelist. In his inspiring book, *Adventures in Two Worlds*, he tells of an experience he had while still a practicing physician.

He was attending a man, a public figure in a northern town who had all his life prided himself upon his atheism. This man had quarrelled with his only daughter and disowned her because she married a schoolmaster who was devoutly religious. Toward the end of his life, when stricken by an incurable malady, a strange change came over this old skeptic. Since death's shadow lay painfully upon him, he became almost passionate in seeking to justify himself in the eyes of his son-in-law. He wasn't inclined to change, but obviously wanted some relationship. Cronin writes:

Time and time again he would wander round to his daughter's home to engage the younger man in argument.

If he wavered he did not show it, for always he concluded with the remark:

"Don't delude yourself. I'm not repentant. I still don't believe in God."

To which one day his daughter, by a stroke of genius, replied: "But Father, He believes in you."

This simple remark swept away the last of the old man's resistance. And it is indeed a thought which might serve for all of us. Whatever we may think, whatever we may do, we are still God's children. He is waiting for us. And it takes only one word of faith to acknowledge Him. (Cronin, p. 326-327).

It is not likely that we are going to be loving persons unless we are loved. We are certainly not going to be sustained in loving the Jesus way unless we stay aware of the fact that we are God's children and God loves us.

Reflecting and Recording

Can you recall the occasion, or the time frame of your life, when you became confident that God loved you? Probe your memory and make some notes here about that experience. How old were you? What were the circumstances? Where were you? What persons were involved in either sharing, communicating, or helping you to interpret that love?

Sing aloud the children's song, "Jesus Loves Me, This I Know."

During the Day

During your moments alone throughout the day, sing aloud, "Jesus Loves Me."

If you are not in places where you can sing aloud, maybe you can hum it. At least sing the song in your mind.

Day Two

I AM LOVED, I AM TO BE LOVING

For this is the message you have heard from the beginning, that we should love one another. We must not be like Cain who was from the evil one and murdered his brother. And why did he murder him? Because his own deeds were evil and his brother's righteous. Do not be astonished, brothers and sisters, that the world hates you. We know that we have passed from death to life because we love one another. Whoever does not love abides in death. All who hate a brother or sister are murderers, and you know that murderers do not have eternal life abiding in them. We know love by this, that he laid down his life for us—and we ought to lay down our lives for one another. How does God's love abide in anyone who has the world's goods and sees a brother or sister in need and yet refuses to help?"

—1 John 3:11-17

A. J. CRONIN, IN HIS *ADVENTURES IN TWO WORLDS*, shares another story:

Some years ago in London, where I had in my spare time organised a working boys' club, I invited a distinguished zoologist to deliver an evening lecture to our members. His was a brilliant address, although to my concern rather different from what I had expected. Acting no doubt on the idea that youth should be told "the truth," my friend chose as his subject "The Beginning of Our World." In a frankly atheistic approach he described how, aeons and aeons ago, the pounding prehistoric seas upon the earth's primaeval crust had generated by physiocochemical reaction a pulsating scum from which there had emerged—though he did not say how—the first primitive form of animation, the protoplasmic cell. It was strong meat for lads who had been brought up on a simpler diet. When he concluded there was polite applause. In the somewhat awkward pause that followed, a mild and very average youngster rose nervously to his feet.

"Excuse me, sir." He spoke with a slight stammer. "You've explained how these b-big waves beat upon the shore; b-b-but how did all that water get there in the first place?"

The naïve question, so contrary to the scientific trend of the address, took everyone by surprise. There was a silence. The lecturer looked annoyed, hesitated, slowly turned red. Then, before he could answer, the whole club burst into a howl of laughter. The elaborate structure of logic offered by this test-tube realist had been crumpled by one word of challenge from a simple-minded boy (Cronin, p. 324).

There is an argument, though, and a rather clear logic about the dynamic of our relationship to God: Because I am loved, I am to be loving.

How do we know we are Christian, that Christ abides in us? John puts it clearly: "We know that we have passed from death to life because we love one another. Whoever does not love abides in death" (1 John 3:14).

Dr. E.V. Hill, a dynamic African-American pastor, serves a church in the Watts area of Los Angeles. Back in the sixties, when horrible riots broke out in that section of the city, he showed his courage. From his own pulpit he denounced his neighbors who were burning and destroying property and stealing from the merchants. This brought all kinds of threats against him as a person.

Late one night, the telephone rang. There was something about the way Hill held the receiver that told his wife something was wrong. When he hung up, she wanted to know who had called and what they wanted. Hill didn't want to talk. She persisted, almost demanding that he tell her.

Finally he did. "I don't know who it was," he said, "but they've threatened to blow up my car with me in it." Throughout the night, Hill was restless and uneasy. He couldn't sleep for the longest time, worrying about the threat to his life. Finally his drowsiness caught up with him and he did fall asleep about 2:00 A.M.

At seven in the morning he awakened terrified. He reached over to touch his wife and she was gone. He couldn't find her anywhere in the house. He then looked out the window to see if she had gone outside. To his greater horror she wasn't on the patio or in the yard. He then realized the car was gone from the carport. He was beside himself and was about to call the police when he saw her turn in the driveway and park the car in the carport.

"Where have you been!" he almost shouted at her.

Do you know what she said?

"I just wanted to drive the car around the block to make sure it was safe for you this morning."

"From that day on", said Dr. Hill, "I have never asked my wife if she loved me!" (Neaves, May 13, 1989)

What a picture! Mrs. Hill was paying attention to Jesus. "We know love by this, that he laid down his life for us—and we ought to lay down our lives for one another" (1 John 3:16).

I can imagine that not only did Dr. Hill never ask his wife whether she loved him or not, but his love for her took on a deeper intensity and a more deliberate expression.

Reflecting and Recording

Yesterday you were asked to recall the experience of becoming aware that you were loved by God. Now locate in your memory your most vivid experience of being loved by another person. Describe that experience.

Spend some time pondering this question: Am I loving with the kind of love called for by my experience of being loved by God and by another?

During the Day

A line of a familiar hymn goes, "O to grace how great a debtor daily I'm constrained to be." Grace is love; love is grace.

Frank Laubach taught us what he called the "flash prayer." This was his way of "praying without ceasing." Let all sorts of occasions—a car horn, the telephone ring, a stop sign, or anything else—be a call to utter a flash prayer. Practice this today and let your prayer simply be the exclamation, "O, to love how great a debtor, daily I'm constrained to be."

Day Three

KEEPING PERSPECTIVE ON OURSELVES

I LIKE PHILLIP'S TRANSLATION OF A PART OF FIRST CORINTHIANS 13:4. Love is "neither anxious to impress, nor does it cherish inflated ideas of its own importance." This has a rather modern ring when compared to the King James Version: "Love vaunteth not itself, is not puffed up."

C. H. Dodd was for many years a professor of biblical studies at Cambridge. He wrote a number of books on biblical studies—a classic on the parables, and another on Paul's teaching, entitled *According to Paul.* Dodd's imperious attitude toward his students and faculty colleagues set him apart in a kind of Olympian detachment, and prompted an oft-repeated limerick in the halls of Cambridge.

> I deem it exceedingly odd,
> that a bumptious old fellow named Dodd
> should spell, if you please, his name with two D's,
> when one is sufficient for God.

We can accept the humor of this and pray that it was a playful heckling of one who might have been a bit puffed up. But there are plenty of instances where the delusion and pretense, false self-perception—having inflated ideas about our own importance—has had tragic and disastrous outcomes. Adolf Hitler in Nazi Germany, Jim Jones in San Francisco and Guyana, Saddam Hussein in Iraq, David Koresh of the Branch Davidians in Waco, Texas. The self-perception of these individuals worked havoc in the world, and led to their own self-destruction.

To love the Jesus way is to love enough to keep ourselves in perspective.

Some time ago, Ned McWherter, governor of Tennessee, showed an admirable side of himself in a brief anecdote which he shared in the newspaper. He said it was easy enough to get puffed up about being the governor of the state of Tennessee, but luckily, Tennesseans have a keen ability to keep "greatness" in perspective. He then told about an experience he had after his election as governor. He went down to his rural hometown of Dresden. From a store on the main street, an elderly gentleman called to him. "Ned? Ned? is that you?" Ned allowed that it was, and the old man invited him in and proceeded to say that he had been seeing the governor a lot on TV and in the newspapers. McWherter confessed with some pride that this was true. Then the old man responded, "Well, I guess you've done pretty well for yourself. But just remember one thing: No matter how rich or successful you become, the number of people at your funeral will still depend a hell of a lot on the weather."

That's right on target, isn't it? To love the Jesus way is to love enough to keep ourselves in perspective. And that means to be humble. Paul pictured that humility of Jesus when he wrote to the Philippians:

> Have this mind among yourselves, which is yours in Christ Jesus, who, though he was in the form of God, did not count equality with God a thing to be grasped, but emptied himself, taking the form of a servant, being born in the likeness of men. And being found in human form he humbled himself and became obedient unto death, even death on a cross. Therefore God has highly exalted him and bestowed on him the name which is above every name, that at the name of Jesus every knee should bow, in heaven and on earth and under the earth, and every tongue confess that Jesus Christ is Lord, to the glory of God the Father.
>
> —Philippians 2:5-11

Do you feel the impact of this? Humility is not a denial of our worth—it's a recognition of our worth. The New English Bible renders a part of that passage in this fashion: "The divine nature was His from the first." Jesus did not lack worth; he claimed worth in a unique way. Humility shines forth clearly where personal value is recognized and acknowledged, but it is not a matter of boasting and conceit.

If you pay attention to this passage in Philippians, you will get a clear picture of humility. It is precisely in that Christ "shared the very being of God," yet did not regard his equality to be clutched to himself, that his humility is defined. He voluntarily and deliberately "humbled himself and became obedient unto death, even death on a cross."

Don't miss this key point. The meaning of humility in the Christian's vocabulary is not in total agreement with the ordinary dictionary definition of the word. In Christian humility there is strength, not weakness. It was possible for Christ to be humble, to take upon himself the form of a servant—washing the disciples' feet, for example—because he had a sense of his own worth, and was aware that he had come from the Father. Jesus knew who he was and therefore he could act as he did.

To love the Jesus way is to love enough to keep ourselves in perspective, and this means to be humble.

Reflecting and Recording

Name three people whom you would describe as humble.

1. _____

_____

2. _____

_____

3. _____

_____

Now beside each name make some notes about these persons. How do they relate to you and other persons? How do they see their job or vocation? How do they function in the family? What is their attitude about money? about power? about education? Do this now.

Look at yourself in light of these persons. What are the likenesses? differences? What does this say about your self-perception? your humility?

During the Day

Continue to use "flash prayers": "O to love how great a debtor, daily I'm constrained to be."

Day Four

LOVE DOES NOT INSIST ON ITS OWN WAY

LOVE SLAPS SELFISHNESS SOLIDLY IN THE FACE—it "does not insist on its own way" (1 Cor. 13:5). This kind of love is willing for the world to turn without one's having to be the center.

I'm pained by the selfish game many baseball players are playing with their names. I'm sure you have been reading about these, even if you have not participated in them—autograph parties for star baseball players. Such players often get $10,000 for an autograph signing party. They get ten, fifteen, or even thirty dollars for each autographed card.

It all seems to have started about ten years ago, when a wily St. Louis entrepreneur started the craze for trading baseball cards, and turned the enhanced value of a card that has been autographed into a business profit. Now, across the land, young boys line up, pay the fee, and file past their hero, who may not even look up. Promoters of these extravaganzas discourage smiles and banter, because it slows the line and cuts the take. Somewhere I read that some stars such as Mike Schmidt, lately of the Phillies, and Orel Hershiser of the Dodgers, still autograph cards the old-fashioned way, *for nothing*. Gary Carter of the Mets asks that you contribute to the Leukemia Society. These players treat their fans not only to a bargain, but also to a lesson in character. Here is a lesson that says some folks are willing for the world to turn without their being the center.

Alan Paton, the South African novelist, once said that the key question for the Christian is not "Am I saved?" but "Am I giving?"

I'm not sure I would put it just that way, but there's no question about it—if you want to test your salvation, test your giving. If you are not growing in your giving—not just of your money, but of your time and talent, of your whole self—then you might well question your Christian experience.

Our model is always Jesus:

I do not say this as a command, but I am testing the genuineness of your love against the earnestness of others. For you know the generous act of our Lord Jesus Christ, that though he was rich, yet for your sakes he became poor, so that by his poverty you might become rich.

—2 Corinthians 8:8-9

The bottom line, then, is the call to give ourselves—to commit ourselves to Jesus Christ as Savior and Lord. This moves us to a lifestyle of giving, because he has given to us.

There is a special call from Jesus to his followers to love those who are cut off from the mainstream of life—the poor, widows, orphans—those who are marginalized. The leper was one such person for Jesus. Jesus called lepers "the least of these." For us it may be a single parent, an unadoptable orphan, an addict, a homosexual. It may be an elderly person in a nursing home, who is without family or is neglected by family. It may be a person of ethnic origin in our neighborhood.

We give—we love—because we have been loved.

Reflecting and Recording

Think back over the past month. What is the most extravagant gift you gave? To whom was it given? What were the circumstances? What led you to do it? Make some notes that give the information about the giving, but also your feelings in the giving.

Contemplating that gift, consider these questions.

To what degree was the gift unselfish?

How much of your *self* was involved in the giving—your time, energy, talent?

What does that gift say about the way you would like to live and relate to others?

During the Day

Pay attention to your attitudes and actions today. How often do you project yourself as the center of the world?

Also, find an occasion to give yourself unselfishly to another (your time, resources, concern) who is marginalized from the mainstream of life, such as those we mentioned above.

Day Five

LOVE DOES NOT KEEP A RECORD OF WRONGS

I READ RECENTLY OF A MAN who was telling a companion about an argument he had had with his wife. "Oh, how I hate it," he said, "every time we fight, she gets historical."

"You mean hysterical," replied the friend. "No, I mean historical," he insisted. "She digs up everything from the past, reminds me of it, and holds it against me."

We know about this, don't we? But such is not the way of love. Love does not keep a record of wrongs.

Verse 6 of 1 Corinthians 13 says, love "does not rejoice in wrongdoing, but rejoices in the truth." That's the New Revised Standard Version. Phillips translates it: "Love does not keep account of evil or gloat over the wickedness of other people. On the contrary, it shares the joy of those who live by the truth."

Let's face it. Few of us are without guilt here. Now and again we find ourselves taking pleasure in other people's sins, gloating over the wickedness of other people. We express this in the way we talk about other people's failures.

In our city not long ago, during the course of one week, the news revealed that one of our African-American political leaders was accused of taking bribes. During the same week, the news told of the dramatic business failure of one of the city's wealthiest white men. It was strange to hear expressions of delight and satisfaction in relation to both. Aware of the racism that poisons us, I was not unduly surprised about the response of some white persons to the politician. But the subtle delight of the white people in the financial problems of another of their own race showed that gloating over others' failures goes beyond race.

James Moffatt translated a part of verse 6 in this fashion, "Love is never glad when others go wrong." Love does not stir around in the muddy waters of maliciousness. It's unfortunate—but our tongues so often betray our Christian profession. Elbert Hubbard once said, "Gossip is a vice enjoyed vicariously." We may not engage directly in the forms of evil that are being talked about, but we listen and witness the gossip, and it seems to pander to our baser passions.

Reflecting and Recording

Try for a few minutes to honestly assess the degree to which you have taken delight when things go wrong for others. Is delight too strong a word? Think about it in this way. Have you had feelings that were far less than sad when things went wrong with others?

During the Day

Remember Hubbard's word, "Gossip is a vice enjoyed vicariously." Guard against that vice today.

Day Six

LOVE IS NOT RESENTFUL

Be still before the Lord, and
wait patiently for him;
do not fret over those who
prosper in their way,
over those who carry out evil
devices.

Refrain from anger,
and forsake wrath.
Do not fret—it leads only to evil.
For the wicked shall be cut off,
but those who wait for the
LORD shall inherit the land.

—Psalm 37:7-9

RESENTMENT IS POISONOUS TO A PERSON. Resentment can become a passion, and when it does it can consume us.

Resentment and anger are intimately connected. We may say resentment is the simmering side-dish of anger. Psychologists tell us that more often than not, resentment is suppressed anger.

The psalmist knew nothing about modern psychology, but he obviously knew about anger and resentment. "Do not fret—it leads only to evil." Many biblical writers were aware of the destructive havoc anger and resentment play in our lives:

Whoever is slow to anger has great understanding, but one who has a hasty temper exalts folly.

—Proverbs 14:29

Be angry but do not sin; do not let the sun go down on your anger.

—Ephesians 4:26

Paul had illuminating insight. I always share his counsel to the Ephesians with the couples I marry. If we let the "sun go down on our wrath," it is likely to smolder inside even unawares, until something sets it off and a volcanic eruption of anger surprises us.

We actually need to see anger as a friend. Anger may be the messenger that tells us something is wrong. Instead of paying anger the attention it deserves, too many of us blow off steam in all sorts of ways, or strike out in hurtful ways. We need to see anger as a red flag, a warning that we should find out what's really going on.

It's interesting that in his description of love, Paul said nothing about anger. We've falsely assumed that anger and love cannot go together. Anger is not an enemy of love; but resentment is.

Indira Gandhi colorfully expressed an obvious truth: "You can't shake hands with a closed fist." Commenting on this in a daily meditation for May 10 in *Believing in Myself*, Ernie Larsen and Carol Hagarty have said:

Are you one who keeps a list? Many of us take very careful count of all that has been lost. With the scrupulous exactitude of resentment, we tally up every wrong that was done to us, every privilege or pleasure that we were denied, every hardship or obstacle that blocked our way. Because we make such an effort to record everything, our list grows and grows with each passing year. And the longer it gets, the better we like it. Justifying resentments can be mighty satisfying.

The problem is that list making keeps us fixated at the point of our losses. It nails us to the past, forever victimized, forever on the lookout for more of the same.

Resentment closes the hand to a fist. How can a fist reach out in friendship or reconciliation? How can a fist receive love or any other gift? A fist may be fine for clutching a grubby little pencil and slashing away at a yellowing old score card. But it closes off too many good things. Nobody ever *gave* anything to a fist.

As we check on our love life, we need to check on our resentments.

Reflecting and Recording

Complete the following four sentences.

1. I resent _____

2. I resent _____

3. I resent _____

4. I resent _____

How long did it take you to finish those four sentences? What does that say about resentment in your life?

I deliberately did not give you fuller instructions about completing the sentences. Did you assume I was asking you to name persons? Think about it. We may resent our job, our neighborhood. We may resent the weather. Spend some time thinking about the different resentments in your life and their dangers.

During the Day

When anger comes on today, count to ten—not to repress your anger, but to question what red flag is being waved over your life and what you need to do about it.

Day Seven

LOVE REJOICES IN TRUTH

Have mercy on me, O God,
according to your steadfast love;
according to your abundant mercy
blot out my transgressions.

Wash me thoroughly from my iniquity,
and cleanse me from my sin.

For I know my transgressions,
and my sin is ever before me.
Against you, you alone, have I sinned,
and done what is evil in your sight,
so that you are justified in your sentence
and blameless when you pass judgement.
Indeed I was born guilty,
a sinner when my mother conceived me.

You desire truth in the inward
being;
therefore teach me wisdom in
my secret heart.

—Psalm 51:1-6

PAUL REMINDS US OF THE CONNECTION BETWEEN LOVE AND TRUTH. Love "does not rejoice in wrongdoing, but rejoices in the truth" (1 Cor. 13:6). The psalmist connects "truth in the inward being," and "wisdom in my secret heart."

Playing with truth is like playing with fire. The temptation to hide the truth is strong, because truth is often painful.

Love rejoices in truth because love affirms the person. So telling the truth begins with seeking the truth about ourselves and boldly facing that truth. Carl Jung said, "Everything that irritates us about others can lead to an understanding of ourselves."

Out of seeking the truth about ourselves, we may come to the point where our speaking will be totally truthful. This is the place truth is often tested—in our speaking. Somewhere along the way I came across a prayer which I try to remember to pray daily. "Lord, make my words sweet and tender today, for I may have to eat them tomorrow."

Have you ever had to eat your words?

You verbalized suspicions that were unfounded.
You shared rumors that were untrue.
You accused someone hastily because you misjudged his motives.

You misunderstood what a person was saying, and you lashed
   back in anger.
You passed on a rumor only to discover it was blatantly false.

Words can hurt, even destroy. And words can hurt *us* when we have
to eat them. Maybe you would like to join me in praying, "Lord, make
my words sweet and tender today, for I may have to eat them tomorrow."
Love rejoices in truth.

Reflecting and Recording
Read again the list above that begins with "You verbalized suspicions. . . ."

Have you spoken words you had to eat recently? Do you need to
apologize to someone and/or ask forgiveness?

During the Day
The following Kenyan Prayer is printed on page 159. Cut it out and
put it some place where you will see it and be reminded to pray it.

From the cowardice that dares not face new truths,
From the laziness that is content with half-truths,
From the arrogance that thinks it knows all truths,
Good Lord, deliver me.

GROUP MEETING FOR WEEK FOUR

Introduction
Paul advised the Philippians to "let your conversation be as it
becometh the gospel" (Phil. 1:27, KJV). The Elizabethan word for *life* as
used in the King James Version is *conversation*, thus Paul's word to the
Philippians. Life is found in communion with God and also in conversation with others. Most of us have yet to see the dynamic potential of
the conversation that takes place in an intentional group such as this.
   To listen is an act of love. When we listen in a way that makes a

difference, we surrender ourselves to the other person, saying, "I will hear what you have to say and will receive you as I receive your words." When we speak in a way that makes a difference, we speak for the sake of others; thus we are contributing to the process of wholeness.

Speaking and listening with the sort of deep meaning that communicates life is not easy. This week our emphasis has been on assessing our love life. These things are not easy to talk about. Therefore, careful listening and responding to what we hear this week in the group meeting is very important.

Sharing Together

1. Invite three or four willing persons to share the experience when they became confident that God loved them (Day One).

2. Invite two or three persons to share their most vivid experience of being loved by another.

3. Spend five to ten minutes discussing love and humility— how one of the ways love works in our lives is to make us humble. Love is neither anxious to impress, nor does it cherish inflated ideas of its own importance. Use your reflection on persons you named as humble on Day Three to give your discussion concreteness.

4. Invite two or three volunteers to share their most extravagant gifts given during the past month.

5. In light of the experiences of giving just shared, spend ten to fifteen minutes talking about the need to give ourselves unselfishly in love to
   — elderly people in our family or neighborhood;
   — the poor—be specific in your consideration—not the poor in general, but particular poor people;
   — marginalized persons such as homosexuals, addicts.

6. Spend a bit of time discussing the ministry of the church of which you are a part in view of the call to give ourselves unselfishly in love.

7. Spend a few minutes examining the fact that there is an aspect of our nature that rejoices, or is tempted to rejoice, in the failure or misfortune of another. What is the weakness or motivation that causes this?

8. Discuss the assertion made on Day Six that *resentment*, not *anger*, is an enemy of love.

Praying Together

Corporate prayer is one of the great blessings of the Christian community. To affirm it is one thing; to experience it is another. To *experience* it we have to *experiment* with the possibility. Will you be a bit bolder now and experiment with the possibilities of corporate prayer by sharing more openly and intimately?

1. Let as many persons who will, share a love need in their life:
   — a need to be loved;
   — a failure to love another;
   — an unwillingness to take the risk of loving the least of these;
   — or, a burdensome, unresolved resentment.
2. Now, have a period of corporate prayer, with as many people as are willing to offer verbal prayers for those who have shared specific needs and/or concerns.
3. Sing a chorus or a verse of a hymn everyone knows, such as "Amazing Grace," "He Is Lord," or "Jesus Loves Me."
4. Hugging is a good expression of love. You may want to hug some folks as you close the meeting.

WEEK FIVE

Loving
Closeup

PATIENCE

Love is patient; love is kind; love is not envious or boastful or arrogant or rude. It does not insist on its own way; it is not irritable or resentful; it does not rejoice in wrongdoing, but rejoices in the truth. It bears all things, believes all things, hopes all things, endures all things.

—1 Corinthians 13:4-7

IN THESE FOUR VERSES PAUL GIVES A PROFOUND distillation of the elements, or characteristics of love.

Henry Drummond, in *The Greatest Thing in the World*, used the image of taking a beam of light and passing it through a crystal prism. The light comes out blue, yellow, violet, orange—and all the other shades of the rainbow. So, Paul passes love through "the magnificent prism of his inspired intellect, and it comes out on the other side broken up into its elements."

Here are the essential characteristics of love that we need in closeup relationships.

Let's begin where Paul begins. Love is *patient. Nothing is more essential for loving closeup than patience.*

There is the story of a man who was determined to revitalize the romance in his marriage. He normally left his factory job sweaty and dirty, went home, entered by the back door, took a beer out of the refrigerator, and sat down to read the paper and watch TV until dinner. But on this particular night, he was determined to let his wife know that he was still very much in love with her. He showered and shaved before he left work. He dressed in some clean and sporty clothes. He was determined to do what a lover might do, so he stopped at a florist and bought flowers, went to the front door, rang the doorbell, and waited for his wife to answer. When she opened the door, he held out the flowers and said, "Honey, I love you."

She took one look at the flowers, then at him, and burst into tears. "Oh, I've had a horrible day. Billy broke his leg and I rushed him to the hospital. Just as I got home, the phone rang. It was your mother, and she's coming for two weeks. I tried to catch up on some laundry and the washer broke down. There's water all over the basement floor, and now you've come home drunk!"

Sometimes even our best-intentioned efforts are missed by those we love. Patience is needed by those who live in closeup relationships, especially marriage.

What enables us to cope with the contentious characters some of our mates turn out to be? Lately I've been reading the Proverbs during my time of morning devotion. Recently I came to the twenty-first chapter. The Book of Proverbs is a lot of pungent sayings connected together without much theme. I came to the ninth verse, which said, "Better to live in a corner of the housetop than in a house shared with a contentious woman." Well, I dwelt on that for a while and read on—and do you know what? When I got to the nineteenth verse, the thought recurred again. That verse says, "Better to dwell in the *a desert land* than with a contentious and fretful wife."

Now that's tough on women. In other places the writer of Proverbs is very tough on men. When he talked about fools he referred to men. I ask you, what enables us to cope with the contentious characters some of our mates turn out to be? What enables us to be calm in the midst of the confusion three children bring to any household? What provides us clarity of perspective and consistency of commitment when the circumstances swirling around our household are so chaotic and trying? The answer to all these questions is *patience.*

Reflecting and Recording

On a scale of 1 to 10, with 1 being the lowest and 10 being the highest, how do you rate yourself in terms of patience?

1	2	3	4	5	6	7	8	9	10

Who is the person with whom you are most impatient? Name that person here. _____

What is it about that person that makes you impatient? Make some notes.

Reflect for a few moments on these questions.

Am I more impatient with persons I love and I am close to than with persons I am with often, but have no love bond?

In relation to the person I named above, do I love her/him enough to work on being more patient?

During the Day

Pay attention to your *patience quotient*. Try to track the circumstances and persons that tax your patience. See if there is a pattern you can adjust in order to express more love.

Day Two

LOVE LOOKS FOR A WAY TO BE CONSTRUCTIVE

This love of which I speak is slow to lose patience—it looks for a way of being constructive. It is not possessive: it is neither anxious to impress nor does it cherish inflated ideas of its own importance.

Love has good manners and does not pursue selfish advantage. It is not touchy. It does not keep account of evil or gloat over the wickedness of other people. On the contrary, it shares the joy of those who live by the truth.

—1 Corinthians 13:4-7, PHILLIPS

IN MOST TRANSLATIONS, THE SECOND CHARACTERISTIC OF LOVE named by Paul is *kindness*. "Love is patient; love is kind." The New King James Version has it, "Love suffers long and is kind." J. B. Phillips adds illumination with his translation: "[Love] looks for a way to be constructive."

How we need this dynamic in living and loving closeup! At the heart of the meaning of kindness is "the desire to bless someone with good." How far we have been from a strong understanding of this word. *Kindness* is a weak word for many of us; or, to be more precise, we have a weak understanding of kindness. It means that we are to be gentle, accepting, understanding—not rough or challenging or demanding. We associate it as much with tenderness as anything else. And it is that— tenderness—but it is more. It is the desire to *bless someone with good*.

I remember the awful devastation of Hurricane Andrew in Florida and Louisiana in August of 1992. The variety of human response was amazing. The looting necessitated the call of National Guard troops. But there was another expression of selfishness and greed that could not be controlled. Seeing the opportunity of a "fast buck," outsiders brought in chain saws and generators to sell at five times their true value. Ice and bottled water brought exorbitant prices.

In the midst of that greed, one act of selfless love made the news. An African-American man brought in a truckload of crushed ice and gave it away. His comment was, "Sharing is the only way to get through times like these."

No wonder Phillips gave that fresh nuance to this dimension of love: "Love looks for a way to be constructive." This means we initiate, not just respond or react.

Kindness, as an expression of love, calls for intentional action. In relationships, we don't hang back until the other makes the move—we take the initiative.

Reflecting and Recording

List members of your immediate family, and/or your closest friends, on the lines below.

_____

_____

_____

_____

_____

Look now at each name. Is there some way you can be kind by finding a way to be constructive? Make notes beside each name.

During the Day

Carry out some of the things you outlined above.

Hopefully, you have memorized 1 Corinthians 13:1-3 as you were asked to do during Week Two. First Corinthians 13:4-7 is printed on page 159. Cut it out and carry it with you during this week—in your pocket or purse, on the dash of your car—so that you can prayerfully consider it often and memorize it. As you work on memorizing these verses, add them to 1 Corinthians 13:1-3 so that you can keep the entire passage in mind.

Day Three

LOVE EXPRESSES ITSELF IN GOOD MANNERS

A STORY HAS IT THAT NAPOLEON WAS ONCE TOLD that French literature was showing signs of decay under his regime. France needed a creative renaissance. "So," said the emperor, "I will speak to the Minister of Interior about it."

Could Napoleon have been serious? Creative literature from a department of state? Just as frightfully empty, however, is the possibility of reformation of a society that has lost all sense of value, purpose, and meaning.

Phillips's translation of Paul's letter says it well: "Love has good manners and does not pursue selfish advantage. It is not touchy. It does not keep account of evil or gloat over the wickedness of other people. On the contrary, it shares the joy of those who live by the truth."

A lot of this has to do with good old-fashioned manners. In fact, Today's English Version begins verse 5 with this message: "Love is not ill-mannered." It is not in good taste to boast. Arrogance is tacky. To be rude reveals a lack of self-confidence and a woeful lack of appreciation for others. What person who has it together is going to show himself or herself out of control by being irritable or resentful? It just isn't good manners. Love expresses itself in good manners.

I traveled once with one of the most outstanding theologians of this century, a woman of great renown, who has written poetry, hymns, books on Christian doctrine, and has taught in three or four of our nation's leading schools of theology. If I mentioned her name, many would recognize it. We were part of a tour group, and she was a lecturer. She happened to be traveling with the smaller group for which I was responsible. We missed our plane, through no fault of our own, and I was trying to make alternate arrangements. We were in Cypress and I was having difficulty communicating. It was a frustrating, stressful situation. There was some fear involved, because we were stuck in a place that at that time was not too friendly with the United States. Without invitation, my professor friend got involved. I've never seen such rudeness, demanding arrogance, irritability, and resentment on the part of a person as I saw in this supposed model of spirituality and Christian discipleship.

My children were traveling with us, and the girls, Kim and Kerry, were nearby. When my daughter, Kim, later went to Yale Divinity School, she had difficulty reading this theologian's books. Kim remembered the woman's bad manners during that trip.

Reflecting and Recording

As a child, when I would get frustrated, angry, lose control, and act up, my mother would say to me, "Now you're really showing yourself." That's what we do even as adults. When we don't use good manners in closeup relationships, we show ourselves as unloving.

Below is a chart of the day from 6 A.M. to 10 P.M. There are two columns: ME and OTHERS. Walk through yesterday in your mind, hour by hour. In the ME column make notes in the time frame about how you were patient and kind or how you acted ill-manneredly. In the OTHERS column record encounters with others, and how they acted. (I begin with 6 A.M. because many of us are really "bears" early in the morning.)

	ME	OTHERS
6-8 AM		
8-10		
10-12		
12-2 PM		
2-4		
4-6		
6-8		
8-10		

Reflect on what this exercise says about love and good manners.

During the Day

Good manners is the watchword for today. "Thank you," "excuse me," "I'm sorry," "May I help you," are words that need to be spoken. But also pay attention to your body language, the attention you give to others, and the initiative you take in simply expressing good manners.

| *Day Four* |

LOVE IS NOT ARROGANT

I heard a recovering alcoholic say on one occasion, "I had gone through life thinking I was better than everyone and, at the same time, being afraid of everyone." In my relationship with many recovering persons I hear this confession expressed in many different ways.

Having a grandiose image of ourselves isolates us from others and cuts us off from true friendship. This may be a part of our addictive problem.

Amazingly, a person may present an arrogant self, when he or she is actually afraid of others. Sometimes apparent self-confidence is a mask. Many times our arrogance is really a cover-up for fear. Paul said, "love is not arrogant," and John wrote, "there is no fear in love, but perfect love casts out fear (1 John 4:18).

I know firsthand how arrogance and fear work in a relationship. Jerry and I married in 1957. I was young and frightened and falsely confident.

I didn't know it then, but the flower of love is a fragile thing—demanding a lot of attention. It must be watered with intentional honesty and fed with deliberate care, or else it will fade and lose its fragrance.

During the early years of our marriage—perhaps the first seven years—I didn't give the flower of our marriage that kind of attention. I remember a dramatic instance when I almost chopped the flower down. We had been married only a few months, and this was our first conflict. I wasn't prepared to recognize conflict, much less deal with it. I had told myself that to become angry is bad, and to express anger is even worse. I had convinced myself that "mature people" don't get upset—certainly they don't cry! Another illusion of mine was that all ministers have perfect marriages; otherwise they aren't worthy of their profession.

With my distorted *professional* image squeezing in, there was no chance for my *personal* image to emerge: "Preachers don't lose their temper—I'm a preacher—therefore I don't lose my temper."

Jerry hadn't been "schooled" in this kind of control. She came from a family where love was shown in open, physical expressions. Tears and laughter flowed freely. Hugging and kissing were common and feelings were honored.

I married Jerry when she was only a year out of high school. She had not been exposed to preacher images or "preacher wife models." On this occasion, she really expressed herself! I responded calmly, which upset her all the more. Soon she was crying.

"This," I said, "is outrageous." My superior air made Jerry feel like dirt. I stalked out of the bedroom and went downstairs, calling over my shoulder, "When you're ready to discuss this calmly like an adult, I'll be in my study."

I'm sure a big hunk of Jerry died that day, and a big hunk of our relationship died, too. I wasn't alive enough to sense the pain, but Jerry was.

It was years later that I learned just how traumatic that bedroom experience had been for Jerry, and how my failure to accept her as a feeling person had thwarted her personal growth. For years, memories of that encounter shut down the free flow of her feelings. Deep communication was rare.

Thank God, this has changed. It changed because I got my head straight—and my heart right—as far as the expression of love and emotions is concerned. But it changed even more because we have learned to live patiently with one another. If we are going to love closeup, we must let down our guard, trust each other, and fight our arrogance whether it is superficial or real.

Reflecting and Recording

Look at your experience with your spouse, or if you are not married, with the person with whom you share most intimately. Check your arrogance quotient. It may be arrogance that veils insecurity, or insecurity that causes you to act in ways not true to yourself. Fear and the appearance of self-confidence often go together. The confusion of the two leads to attitudes and actions that hurt others. Have there been occasions when you hurt the one you love? Spend five minutes simply thinking about the relationship.

♥

Are there decisions you need to make? Actions you need to take, such as apologizing, asking forgiveness, changing relational patterns?

♥

During the Day

William Law said, "Love has no more of pride than light has of darkness; it stands and bears all its fruit from a depth and root of humility."

This wisdom is printed on page 159. Cut it out and place it in some obvious place, i.e., a refrigerator door, bathroom mirror, the dashboard of your car, in your purse or wallet. Read it as often as you see it and seek to incorporate the humility of loving into your life.

| Day Five |

LOVE DOES NOT INSIST ON ITS OWN WAY

HAVE YOU EVER HAD A WART? Warts are ugly, they irritate, and they serve absolutely no good purpose.

My friend, George Mann, whom I succeeded as pastor of the West Anaheim United Methodist Church in California, provided a very helpful insight in a column he wrote for his church paper. He used the analogy of warts, and he quoted Lewis Thomas, the president of Memorial Sloan-Kettering Cancer Center in New York. Thomas talked about warts in this fashion:

> Warts are wonderful structures. They can appear overnight on any part of the skin, like mushrooms on a damp lawn, full blown and splendid in the complexity of their architecture. Viewed in stained sections under a microscope, they are the most specialized of cellular arrangements, constructed as though for a purpose. They sit there like turreted mounds of dense, impenetrable horn, impregnable, designed for defense against the world.

Isn't this the trend of our culture? We are a wart-like people, taking our stand in defense against everybody else. Warts live off the bodies to which they are attached, yet contribute nothing to the body. The wart is designed for, and lives for, its own being.

Think about two characteristics of wart-like people.

First, *Protection*—defense against everybody else. One of our primary defenses or means of protection is to assume a victim mentality. "Nobody understands me." "I don't deserve this treatment." "He or she must be out to do me in." "My problems are your fault."

Two, *Receiving*—taking everything we can from everyone we can. To offer another image, think of the leech which lives off the blood of another life. That may be too dramatic, but you get the picture.

Wart-like people are caricatures of those who insist on their own way.

In our sinfulness, we humans become wart-like. So Paul says, love must "not insist on its own way." A recurring theme of scripture is selfless living. Jesus made it very clear in his call to discipleship: "Then he said to them all, 'If any want to become my followers, let them deny themselves and take up their cross daily and follow me'" (John 9:23).

One of the failures of the church is that many Christians insist on their own way—the time of worship that is convenient to them, the type of music they think is appropriate for worship (which may have no appeal to non-church people), the order and style of liturgy (using "in-house" specialty language that a person unschooled in Christianity does not understand), the "proper" way to dress, and so on. A great segment of our population either has no Christian memory or is completely secular in orientation. The church is not ever going to speak to these people a message they understand, much less convince them of the validity of the message, as long as we "insist on our own way."

Reflecting and Recording

Take a five-minute look at the last two weeks of your life. In Column One make notes, giving time, persons, and situations where you "insisted on your own way." In Column Two make notes about occasions when you were genuinely loving.

Insisted on My Own Way   **Genuinely Loving**

Write a prayer expressing your own feelings about what you have discovered about yourself in this exercise.

During the Day

Continue to reflect on William Law's wisdom about the humility of love.

[*Day Six*]

LOVE DOES NOT KEEP AN ACCOUNT OF EVIL

Two others also, who were criminals, were led away to be put to death with him. When they came to the place that is called The Skull, they crucified Jesus there with the criminals, one on his right and one on his left.

Then Jesus said, "Father, forgive them; for they do not know what they are doing." And they cast lots to divide his clothing.

—Luke 23:32-34

JESUS' WORD FROM THE CROSS is the ultimate expression of forgiveness. The crowd was railing at him, taunting him, spitting on him as he suffered a horrible death beyond description. For these raucous, calloused persons Jesus prayed, "Father, forgive them, for they do not know what they are doing." Then in an act that must have demanded every ounce of energy left in his agonizing body, he turned his pain-throbbing head in the direction of the penitent thief to offer forgiveness and a promise of life with him in Paradise.

With a memory of that ultimate expression of love, Christians should know the seriousness of Paul's word about love. "Love does not keep an account of evil."

In his poem "Tam O'Shanter," Robert Burns describes a woman waiting for her husband to come home from the inn, as "nursing her wrath to keep it warm."

We do that, don't we? We nurse our wrath. We brood over the wrong that has been done to us. We keep a mental record of how we have been slighted.

Most translations of 1 Corinthians 13 have this phrase, "love is not resentful." The Greek word translated *resentful* is an accountant's term. It means making a note or recording in a ledger, so that it will not be forgotten.

Isn't that what resentment is? It keeps a ledger of hurts, offenses, slights, insults, oversights—things done to us that we are unwilling to forget.

None of us should pass this over lightly. Resentment is a common cause for emotional illness. Holding grudges poisons our minds and souls. Recently, I had a counseling appointment with a seventy-year-old man. He was morbidly depressed. There was no vitality about him. Even his eyes were dim—no sparkle came from any part of him. He poured out feelings of anguishing guilt because he had promised his wife a trip to Europe. She had dreamed and planned for years, but she had died unexpectedly six years ago. He continued to accuse himself, even after six years, for denying his wife the happiness she deserved.

As that man talked, I remembered a woman in a television interview. She had been raped, brutally abused, mutilated, and left to die. She was talking about her astonishing survival, even though the shot that was meant to kill her had left her blind. The television host talked about the emotional scars that she would have to deal with the rest of her life, and asked about her anger and bitterness toward her attacker.

Her answer burned in my mind, almost taking my breath away: "Oh, no. That man took one night of my life. I refuse to give him an additional second."

Unbelievable! Yes, on first hearing. But who is the healthy one? Who is living—really living? The man with whom I was counseling, or this woman?

Grudges, resentment, and refusing to forgive are barriers to life, poison to our souls. Paul knew: "Love does not keep an account of evil." And Jesus gave us the pattern and power for life: "Father, forgive them."

Reflecting and Recording

Muster all the honesty of which you are capable. Name in the blanks below the persons against whom you are carrying a grudge or a resentment; perhaps someone who has wronged you whom you have not forgiven.

_____

_____

_____

_____

_____

Make notes beside each name, giving some detail or describing the action or attitude that brought you to this place. Write enough to get in touch with your feelings.

♥

Now list each of the persons again.

_____

_____

_____

By the name of each person write down what you can do and are willing to do to rid yourself of resentment, to forgive the person and reconcile the relationship.

During the Day

Busy yourself immediately in acting out what you have just written. This is necessary to rid yourself of guilt and resentment.

Day Seven

LOVE NEVER DOES THE GRACE-LESS THING

IN THE KING JAMES VERSION, verse 5 of 1 Corinthians 13 says, "Love doth not behave itself unseemly." Though archaic in its sound, this is intriguing, isn't it? "Love does not behave itself unseemly."

It would be interesting to know just what that phrase conveys to different people. I suspect that, for most, it has a specifically moral "feel" about it. So, being translated into those terms, it would read, "Love is not guilty of immoral behavior."

Dennis Duncan reminds us that the phrase

"immoral behaviour" means, for many a Christian, sexual misbehaviour, for it is the case that, in church circles particularly, that area has been associated—more than any other part of life, with sin. Jesus, on the other hand, consistently drew attention to the much wider and, perhaps really, more serious forms of immoral behaviour—those associated with spiritual pride, envy, intolerance, arrogance, self-righteousness, selfishness, etc. So, whatever "unseemly" behaviour is, it is much more than statutory immoral behaviour. *It has something to say about a person's whole attitude to life and to people* (Duncan, p. 23).

William Barclay has the most helpful rendering of this line. He translates it, "[Love] does not behave gracelessly." Isn't that beautiful? Love never does the graceless thing.

Grace is an almost indefinable word as far as the New Testament is concerned. In our ordinary understanding it has elements of charm and refinement and elegance about it. But in the New Testament sense, it has to do with good will and favor and undeserved benefit at the hands of a loving God—and it means that as we live a life of grace, we are living in a way that blesses and uplifts and transforms and renews others.

Grace reaches down into the very heart of the human struggle, and brings graceful influence on the battle waged in the human soul. Gracelessness pulls down rather than builds up, degrades rather than refines, brings deterioration rather than spiritual improvement. Love can never do "the graceless thing." Love does not abide in attitudes or behaviors that degrade humankind, that afflict or influence human beings in a destructive way. So love is always "on the side of the angels" and will never involve itself in behavior that produces any kind of distrust or destructiveness.

Reflecting and Recording

The gospel hymn "Come Thou Fount of Every Blessing" says it well:

> O to grace how great a debtor
> daily I'm constrained to be!
> Let thy goodness, like a fetter,
> bind my wandering heart to thee.

To be sure, we are debtors to the grace of Jesus Christ. But what about our indebtedness to the grace of other persons? Spend a few minutes remembering and thanking God for persons who have been "all grace" to you.

Reflect on the past week. Write a prayer of confession of the *graceless things* you have done and of thanksgiving for the grace you have received.

During the Day

Continue your prayerful consideration and memorization of 1 Corinthians 13:4-7.

Guard against doing the *graceless thing* today.

GROUP MEETING FOR WEEK FIVE

Introduction

John Wesley called on Christians to use all the "means of grace" available for their Christian walk, their growth in Christlikeness. Along with those means we normally think of—prayer, scripture, study, worship, Holy Communion—Wesley named Christian *conferencing*. By this, he meant intentional Christian conversation—talking about spiritual matters and sharing our Christian walk.

These group sessions provide practice in the art of Christian conferencing. As you share together in the "safe" setting of a group of mutually-committed persons, you are being equipped to share in less safe relationships. Keep this in mind as you share in this session and as you continue your weekly gatherings.

Sharing Together

1. You have finished five weeks of this workbook journey. Spend a few minutes talking about the experience in general terms. What is giving you difficulty? What is providing the most meaning?

2. Spend a few minutes sharing by "confessing our sin" of being more patient with others than with those we love and are close to.

3. Spend about ten minutes talking about "good manners" as an expression of love. Be as honest as possible in assessing your own pattern of relating. Refer to the chart on Day Three.

4. Invite as many as will to share the degree to which they use "self-confidence" to mask their fear.

5. Talk about the congregations of which the persons in the group are a part. To what degree are we failing to reach people outside of the church because we "insist on our own way"?

6. Spend the balance of your time discussing this aspect of love: Love "never does the graceless thing."

Praying Together

Spontaneous conversational prayer—persons offering brief sentences—is a powerful dynamic in group life. One person may offer a sentence or two now, and then again after two or three others have prayed. One person's prayer may suggest another. Don't try to say everything in your one prayer. Pray pointedly, knowing you can pray again during this time of prayer. This way you can be spontaneous and not strain to make sure you have "covered all the bases."

1. Invite those who wish, to share a current situation which is demanding a commitment and perseverance in love. Let two or three in the group offer sentence prayers in response to this sharing.

2. Invite two or three persons to offer prayers of thanksgiving for those who have provided "all-grace" to them (Day Seven).

3. Close now by giving persons the opportunity to share specific prayer requests, and then spend a brief time in spontaneous conversational prayer.

4. Turn the pictures upside down so that each person can take one and pray daily for that person during the upcoming week.

WEEK SIX

A Love
for
All
Seasons

LOVE BEARS ALL THINGS

IN VERSE SEVEN OF 1 CORINTHIANS 13, Paul gives a kind of summary of his description of love. Love "bears all things, believes all things, hopes all things, endures all things." Though a summary, we can pursue more direction for loving the Jesus way by concentrating on the three action words, *bears*, *hopes*, *endures*. Primarily using these words, our theme this week is "a love for all seasons."

Love *bears* all things. It has muscle. It is not morally weak. It is not naïve. It is tough—it doesn't indulgently accept wrong or pretend that wrong does not exist.

Love knows that persons are at stake, and persons have eternal value. There comes the time when loving has to be strong and not bend to pressure. Redemption—not ruination—is the goal of love. For the sake of another, love bears all things.

The philosopher Nikolay Berdyayev was at a concentration camp more than fifty years ago when the Nazis were murdering Jews in the gas chambers. At one point a distraught mother refused to part with her little baby. The officer tussled with her, trying to split them apart because he needed only one more Jew to throw in the gas chamber to fulfill his quota for the day.

And then it happened. Another woman, a simple woman named Maria, realized what was happening. In a flash she pushed the mother and her baby out of the way, and she became the one thrown by the officer into the chamber!

Berdyayev's life was changed from that day forward.

That is a dramatic story, and it raises some questions worthy of reflection. Have we ever seen that kind of love? Have we experienced anything that comes close to that kind of love?

Move from the dramatic. Have we ever demonstrated love so clearly and powerfully that it made a difference in someone's life?

Reflecting and Recording

Spend some time considering the questions raised above. Specifically, locate in your experience the occasions when you came closest to loving in a way that made a difference in someone else's life.

During the Day

"Love bears all things, believes all things, hopes all things, endures all things." Memorize this sentence and take it with you to shape your attitude and responses to others.

Day Two

LOVE COVERS ALL THINGS

THE BIBLICAL SCHOLAR AND TRANSLATOR, James Moffatt, says that the rendering of the Greek word translated "bears" in 1 Corinthians 13:7 could also be "covers." This gives us a picture of love casting a veil over the weakness and failings of others. In reading Proverbs as a part of my daily devotional and prayer time, I've circled those single proverbs that have grabbed my attention. Leafing through the Book of Proverbs recently, I found this pungent truth circled: "Hatred stirs up strife, but love covers all offenses" (Prov. 10:12).

Does this mean that we close our eyes to blatant evil, or make the sloppy response, "he is only doing what everybody else does"? Does it mean that love is not willing to expose the wrongdoing and sin of another?

Not at all! Love is willing even to hurt another, but only for the purpose of inducing healing. Recovering addicts in Twelve Step programs understand this. This kind of loving honesty is mentioned in the November 2 meditation in *Touchstones: Daily Meditations for Men*:

We owe our brothers and sisters in this program our honest feedback. And we need the same honesty from them. There are times in meetings when it would be easiest to give someone sympathy and privately mutter to ourselves, "He isn't facing the bitter truth." That sympathy avoids a confrontation, but it doesn't give the healing medicine of honesty. In the same way, we may long, at times, for someone to give us warm strokes, and what they give instead is a bitter pill.

The most important thing we have to give one another is the truth of what we see and hear. We don't have to tell them what to do. We don't have to have all the right answers. But we do have the obligation to speak up about how things look to us. And we need to listen without defensiveness when others are honest with us.

So, love doesn't "cover" that which needs to be exposed in order for healing to take place. Honesty is stronger than sympathy. Sympathy often conceals, but love does not.

Loves *covers* our faults, weaknesses, and failures; that is, love *accepts*. Love *covers* our sins; that is, love *forgives*.

God deals with us in this manner—accepting our faults, weakness, and failures; forgiving our sins—and God is love. This is the way the prophet Micah saw God:

Who is a God like you, pardoning iniquity and passing over the transgression of the remnant of your possession? He does not retain his anger forever, because he delights in showing clemency. He will again have compassion upon us; he will tread our iniquities under foot. You will cast all our sins into the depths of the sea.

—Micah 7:18-19

Reflecting and Recording

Bill Cosby put an important truth in a quaint way: *Every closed eye is not sleeping, and every open eye is not seeing.* Spend a bit of time thinking about how you may need to close your eyes to some things for love's sake. Also probe a bit about whether you may be hiding from something, though your eyes are apparently open. Sometimes love does not *cover*, it confronts. Is there someone with whom you need to be more honest in sharing what you see and hear that may be hurting them and hindering their relations with others? Spend some time with the question.

Is there someone who especially needs the *cover* of your love? He or she needs to know without a doubt that you accept his or her faults, weakness, and failure; that you forgive. Spend some time with this question.

Pray specifically for the persons you have been thinking about.

During the Day

Don't let this day pass without doing something to let the persons you have been thinking about know your love. Cosby's expression of truth is printed on page 159. If you will fold it on the dotted line, it will become a tent card. You may put it in an obvious place where you will see it often and be challenged. (Where you eat breakfast or on your desk at work are good places.) On the other side are printed the words "Practice random acts of kindness and senseless acts of beauty."

Day Three

LOVE CARRIES

Surely he has borne our
infirmities
and carried our diseases;
yet we accounted him stricken,
struck down by God, and
afflicted.
But he was wounded for our
transgressions,

crushed for our iniquities;
upon him was the punishment
that made us whole,
and by his bruises we are
healed.
All we like sheep have gone
astray;
we have all turned to our own
way,
and the LORD has laid on him
the iniquity of us all.

—Isaiah 53:4-6

Come to me, all you that are weary and are carrying heavy burdens, and I will give you rest. Take my yoke upon you, and learn from me; for I am gentle and humble in heart, and you will find rest for your souls. For my yoke is easy, and my burden is light.

—Matthew 11:28-30

Love *bears* all things. This word has the meanings *to cover* and *to carry*. It also has the meaning of carrying the burden or blame of another on your own shoulders.

The prophet Isaiah saw the Messiah as one who has "borne our infirmities and *carried* our diseases." Isn't this a picture of Jesus? And isn't the meaning of the Cross glimpsed in this ancient prophetic word? Christ has lifted and carries the burden of our sin. His love *carries* us. "Come to me, all you that are weary and are carrying heavy burdens, and I will give you rest" (Matt. 11:28).

One night a man dreamed that he was walking along the beach with the Lord. Many scenes from his life flashed before him. In each one he noticed footprints in the sand. Sometimes there were two sets of footprints, but at other times there was only one. This bothered him, because he noted that during periods of depression, anguish, and sorrow, he could see only a single set. So he prayed in his distress, "You promised me, Lord, that you would walk with me always. But I noticed that during the most trying periods of my life there has been just one set of footprints in the sand. Why, when I needed you most, haven't you been there?"

The Lord replied with love in his eyes, "The times when only one set of footprints were made, my son, were the times that I carried you."

God told the Israelites, "I bore you on eagles' wings" (Exod. 19:4). And again, "The eternal God is your dwelling place, and underneath are the everlasting arms" (Deut. 33:27, RSV).

Love bears all things—willingly carries the burden and blame of another. Are we ready—in the sense of being equipped and able—to love in this fashion? Most of us aren't. We need to deal, not with the question of readiness, but with the question of *willingness*. If we wait until we are ready and able, we will never love as we are called to. Within ourselves we don't have that kind of strength.

There is a challenging story of the nurse who was tending the wounds of a soldier. The soldier had been left out on the field of battle for three days without medical attention. His wounds had not been cleaned, and gangrene had set in. The stench was almost unbearable. A newspaper reporter looking on said, "I wouldn't do that for a million dollars." The nurse responded, "Neither would I!"

The question is not readiness to love but willingness. If we are willing, the Holy Spirit will equip us with this "love for all seasons"— this love that bears all things.

Reflecting and Recording

Return to your reflection yesterday about persons who need to know your love both in the sense of *confronting* and *covering*. Continue to think of those persons today. Does what you have thought about them have anything to do with carrying their burden or blame? Think about this for a while, and then pray for them.

During the Day

If you were not able to show your love to these persons yesterday, seek to do so today.

Day Four

LOVE BELIEVES ALL THINGS

AS I'VE ALREADY SUGGESTED, reading the Bible in different translations often provides additional meaning and unexpected insight to a text. The New Jerusalem Bible offers this translation of 1 Corinthians 13:7—"Love is always ready to make allowances, to trust, to hope and to endure whatever comes."

Ooooh! We don't like this, do we? "Always ready to excuse?" Let's go slowly as we seek to probe the meaning of this.

There's nothing naïve and shallow, nothing pollyannish, about Paul's understanding of love. Trust is the key here. Phillips puts it, "Love knows no end to its trust." Barclay's commentary says love "always believes the best about other people."

Having said this, we still have a problem, and we are compelled to deal with it. How do we keep on believing—trusting—persons?

Dr. William Ritter, a Methodist preacher in Michigan, preached a compelling sermon entitled, "How Many Times Do You Take the Prodigal Back?" which helps us struggle with the issues of belief and trust. His sermon was inspired by a woman who asked the question, "How many times . . . ?" after he had been talking about the prodigal son.

The woman asked this question as she walked out the door following the morning worship service. He knew this woman well enough to know something of the nerve his sermon had struck. She, too, had a son—a son who had been in and out of school, in and out of trouble, in and out of sorts, in and out of the state. The family had taken him back over and over again, had gone to bat for him, had gone with him to counseling, had loaned him money, found him jobs—only to have their home disrupted by his recurring sullen silences or sudden outbursts.

Now, as it turned out, he was home again, arriving as unannounced as he had left. His family never knew when he was coming or going. Therefore, her question, quiet as it was, carried with it the accumulated baggage of a long and painful history: "How many times do you take the prodigal back?" (Ritter, October 16, 1988)

The parable of the prodigal son isn't the complete answer, is it? You remember the story. The young man took all of his part of the family's wealth when he was far too young to take it, and headed off into a far country. He wasted the money and ended up in the gutter. Then he came to himself and realized that even the servants back at his father's house had it better than he. So he said to himself, "I will arise and go to my father, and say to my father, 'I have sinned.'"

This he did. And when he got near the father's house, the father, seeing him, ran down the lane, embraced him, took him back to the house, put a beautiful clean robe on him, shoes on his feet, the signet ring of the family on his finger, and announced that the fatted calf was to be killed and they were going to have a great celebration.

The story stops there—stops with that prodigal son back at home, having been welcomed into the family.

But imagine . . .

What if, on the morning after the big party, the prodigal son heads for the field to lift his share of the load? And what if, after a few sun-drenched days on the business end of a shovel, he says, "Who needs this? This is getting to be a drag." What if he goes off again? Does the story repeat itself? If so, how many times? When does the father begin to get a bit weary of the great return? Does he always run down the road when he sees the boy coming? Does he run as fast the fifth time as he ran the first? Does he ever get to the point where he says: "Oh, no, here we go again."

How many times do you go through the ritual of welcoming? How many robes do you produce from the closet? How many fatted calves do you slaughter? How many rings do you place on how many fingers? How many times do you cry: "This son of mine who was lost has been found; this daughter who was dead is alive again"? How many times do you go down to the police station with bail money? How many times do you pay off a drug dealer who is threatening to break somebody's leg for a couple of hundred dollars? How many counselors do you see? How many attorneys do you hire? How many times do you leave the door unlocked upon going to bed for the night just in case? How many times do you cook oatmeal to nurse how many hangovers? (Ritter)

The story is as new as it is old. Prodigals do return—but they leave again—and they return—and they leave. How many times do you take the prodigal back?

In every congregation I have served as pastor, I could pick at random any twenty couples in my congregation who have children thirteen years and older, take them home with me one day, and after a bit of lunch, we could sit with a glass of tea or a cup of coffee, and tell our prodigal children stories. For some who are older, the prodigal children may have returned home for good. They are grown and home from the far country now and will someday have to deal with their own prodigals. Others are just being introduced to the prodigal syndrome. The signs are just emerging—little forays into the far country, and a quick return—but the leaving again is there, and the parents' heart beats a little faster at the beginning of each weekend. Others are in the painful grip of it, and their story might be even too painful and personal to recount. Prodigals do return, but go again—and the pattern has us not only heartbroken but confused as to what it means to really love.

Such is the story, or stories, that force the question, "How many times? How many times do you take the prodigal back?"

Paul says, "Love bears all things and believes all things," but the question remains, "How many times do you take the prodigal back?"

I do not have an answer that fits every case. But there is one weighty consideration I would have you ponder as you deal with this issue. It carries the weight of the gospel itself. I agree with Dr. Ritter:

Ours is a gospel which errs, if indeed it errs at all, on the side of forgiveness and mercy. Ours is a gospel that is abundantly clear in its counsel toward patience and hope . . . a gospel that talks about second miles to be traveled, cheeks to be turned, and coats to be surrendered along with cloaks . . . a gospel that talks about the need to track down the one who is lost at the expense of the 99 who are saved . . . a gospel that talks about crosses to be borne, enemies to be received, strangers to be embraced, and love that is meant to be string-free . . . a gospel that always sees the pearl of a person's worth within the encrusted shell of that same person's behavior.

To be sure, if the father in Luke's story is meant to be a paradigm for the Heavenly Father, the message is clear. Any imbalance within the love of God is an imbalance which favors last over first, least over most, and the sickest over the one who is well. The Heavenly Father keeps no scrapbook on the number of prodigal-like departures or returns. Praise God for that. Where would the prodigals of this world be without it? Indeed, where would any of us be without it? Would that we could all get it right the first time, or at least the second time.

How we work it out—the number of times we take the prodigal back—will never be easy to decide. But we must always bring the weight of the gospel to our consideration. *Love believes all things.*

Reflecting and Recording

Write a prayer that expresses your own feelings and experiences with the prodigals in your life.

During the Day

Is there some specific action—a letter, a phone call, a word of confrontation, a word of acceptance and forgiveness—you need to take in relation to the prodigals in your life? Begin the process today.

Day Five

LOVE HOPES ALL THINGS

EVERY DISCIPLINE, EVERY SPORT, EVERY ART has its specialized language. In baseball there is a bit of jargon that provides a challenging image. "The runner died on third."

Wouldn't a stranger to baseball have problems with that? Imagine what some person who knew absolutely nothing about baseball would think if he was listening to the radio, and the announcer calling the game said, "And the batter struck out, and Jemison died on third." It's a challenging image because it's suggestive of what happens in life. Because of a lack of love, many a person dies on third. There's no one to share his hope, no one to encourage his dream.

Paul says, "Love hopes all things." Again, another translation speaks to us and brings out the meaning of hope. Barclay provides this insightful rendering: "Love never ceases to hope." That means that love never sees anyone or anything as hopeless.

It has been said that there is a road that leads to Hell even from the gates of Heaven. As true as that might be, it's equally true, and far more comforting, to know that there is a road to Heaven, even from the gates of Hell.

I went to a first birthday party recently, one of the most meaningful celebrations I have experienced. It was not the birthday of a one-year-old. It was the first birthday of sobriety and cleanness for a twenty-six-year-old man.

Fifty or sixty people were there. They came from all walks of life. An outstanding doctor, well known in the city and throughout the medical world for his pediatric research, was there. So was a salesman for cemetery lots, a waitress, and a banker. There was a twenty-three-year-old woman and a sixty-year-old man. The crowd represented every age and every segment of economic, cultural, and social life.

Everyone there was someone who was recovering from an addiction that had almost claimed his or her life, or a person who had prayed for and loved this birthday celebrant through all the years he was in his far country of darkness. Every person there could have given witness to the fact that there is "a road to Heaven, even from the gates of Hell." Love never regards anyone or any situation as hopeless.

The people at that first birthday celebration have a special appreciation for the story of another young man.

But when he came to himself he said, "How many of my father's hired hands have bread enough and to spare, but here I am dying of hunger? I will get up and go to my father, and I will say to him, 'Father, I have sinned against heaven and before you; I am no longer worthy to be called your son; treat me like one of your hired hands.'" So he set off and went to his father. But while he was still far off, his father saw him and was filled with compassion; he ran and put his arms around him and kissed him. Then the son said to him, "Father, I have sinned against heaven and before you; I am no longer worthy to be called your son." But the father said to his slaves, "Quickly, bring out a robe—the best one—and put it on him; put a ring on his finger and sandals on his feet. And get the fatted calf and kill it, and let us eat and celebrate; for this son of mine was dead and is alive again; he was lost and is found!" And they began to celebrate.

—Luke 15:17-24

Reflecting and Recording

Do you have any loved ones or close friends who are in the far country? Don't think only of extremes or dramatic cases. I have a friend who is in the far country of suspicion and fear. She neurotically, often to the point of severity, thinks the "world" is after her. She is frightened and suspicious.

Think of persons who are, to a painful degree, separated from others or from meaning in life. They seem hopeless. Name three of them here.

_____

_____

_____

Have you given up on these persons? Look at each one of them and make some notes about what you might do to express love and offer hope.

During the Day

Continue to be attentive to Cosby's expression of truth: "Every closed eye is not sleeping, and every open eye is not seeing."

If possible reach out to the persons you named who are in the "far country."

Day Six

LOVE ENDURES

IN HIS ONE-SENTENCE SUMMARY which pictures a love for all seasons, Paul said, "Love bears all things, believes all things, hopes all things, endures all things." We now focus our thoughts on the last attribute of love: "[Love] endures all things."

Other translations offer fresh meaning.

The New English Bible: "There is nothing love cannot face; there is no limit to its faith, its hope, and its endurance."

The Jerusalem Bible: "Love . . . endure[s] whatever comes."

The New International Version: "Love always perseveres."

Barclay's translation: "Nothing can happen to break love's spirit."

Stop for a few minutes and reflect on the nuances of the above translations.

Meaning comes to each of us differently, and any nuanced expression may impact one person more than it does another. An eight-year-old girl, after listening attentively to a sermon, wrote, "Dear Pastor, I know God loves everybody, but he never met my sister." Meaning comes according to our experience.

As we consider the notion that love endures all things, and the expression of that idea in these different translations, some of us would think of *tough* love.

On Day Four we looked at the question, "How many times do we take the prodigal back home?" In response to that question we considered the possibility that if love errs, it errs on the side of patience and forgiveness. I closed our study yesterday with a part of the story of the prodigal son, emphasizing the notion that the gospel is certainly weighed on the side of hope. Still, the question remains, how many times do you take the prodigal back?

Love is to be tough, but *how tough*?

Tough Love has been developed as a therapeutic philosophy of family interaction. Tough Love groups meet all over our city every week. I have participated in such groups, in which parents sharing similar stresses with their children wrestle primarily with the "no" dimension of love. William Ritter has provided a description of these groups, to which those who have participated can say, "Yeah, that's it!"

These are people who are undergoing similar stress and need the support of others, need to have that empathetic ear that will hear them out, need to learn from other people's successes and failures. In that kind of fellowship, they receive the strength and courage to take tough stands which enable them to say "No" to an erring son, daughter, or spouse. "No, you will not bring our homes . . . our lives . . . our sanity . . . our pocket-books . . . and our fragile hold on health to ruin by your repeated choices of deviant and destructive behavior." (No, you will not use us, your parents and brothers and sisters, to feed your selfish ego and your refusal to take responsibility. You will not make us sick by your own sickness.) It is in such groups that people often find the courage to lock the doors, tighten the purse strings, and break the patterns which threaten, if unchecked, to fracture families and futures" (Ritter, October 16, 1988).

Somewhere in the dynamic of a Tough Love group, as in other groups such as Twelve-Step, we have to face the question, "Who is sick and who is well?"

Ritter is again lucid on this theme:

By the time a family has paid out $100,000 to drug dealers through the hands of an addicted son or daughter, who can say any longer who is sick and who is well?

By the time a marriage is in the divorce courts because an adolescent has become a source of turmoil, anarchy and even violence in the home, who can say any longer who is sick and who is well?

By the time a family is on its third psychiatrist and second attorney because of the actions of one of its members, who can say any longer who is sick and who is well?

By the time the prodigal has departed and returned so many times that there are no longer any robes, shoes, rings, fat calves (or any calves, for that matter) from which to construct a half-decent party, who can say any longer who is sick and who is well?

By the time the wife of an alcoholic has spent years going around the house finding bottles . . . throwing out bottles . . . lying to friends . . . canceling dinner invitations at the last minute . . . calling the boss and telling him that her husband won't be in because he has the flu . . . all the while secretly believing that if she were a better wife, kept a cleaner house, cooked better meals, kept the kids quieter when he came home, made love more often, lost 20 pounds, and bought some sexy new underwear from Frederick's of Hollywood . . . that he would suddenly stop drinking and come straight home from work—then I ask you, who can say any longer who is sick and who is well?

There is no clear and easy answer. In all settings and certainly in Tough Love and Twelve-Step groups, we may get sanctions for unhealthy angry reactions, sanctions for hardened responses, encouragement to take too quickly steps of last resort, promotion of dogmatic no-saying rather than open dialogue. And this is where balance must come. So, we're back to this amazing affirmation of Paul: Love *endures* all things.

However we deal with those seemingly hopeless situations and persons, and however helpless we may feel, we have to keep working at it in the framework of love as the ultimate commitment and the definition of relationship.

It will challenge us to remember these different expressions:
"There is no limit to love's endurance."
"Love endures whatever comes."
"Love always perseveres."
"Nothing can happen to break love's spirit."

Reflecting and Recording
Go back to the list of persons you made yesterday. Spend some time with this question: What does "tough love" require of me in relation to them?

♥

During the Day

Memorize these four expressions of enduring love:

"There is no limit to love's endurance."

"Love endures whatever comes."

"Love always perseveres."

"Nothing can happen to break love's spirit."

Use these affirmations as "flash scripture" during the day.

Day Seven

BECOMING AS A LITTLE CHILD

People were bringing even infants to him that he might touch them; and when the disciples saw it, they sternly ordered them not to do it. But Jesus called for them and said, "Let the little children come to me, and do not stop them; for it is to such as these that the kingdom of God belongs. Truly I tell you, whoever does not receive the kingdom of God as a little child will never enter it."

—Luke 18:15-17

HAVE YOU NOTICED THAT NEW CHRISTIANS have an almost naïve, childlike openness to God? They expect God to act in their lives, and God does! We lose this childlike faith as we become more knowledgeable, more sophisticated in the faith. What a pity!

My colleague, Norman Neaves, tells of a couple from back east who were over in Arkansas looking at a piece of resort property, a condominium that was elegantly furnished. The salesman took them from one room to the next, showing them first this amenity and then that. Finally, he came to the bathroom. "Now, just look at this," he said proudly showing them the over-sized spacious area, "isn't this something?" And then he pointed to the jacuzzi over in the corner. "And look at that little dude over there," he said. "Have you ever seen anything like it before?" The fellow from back east said, "Wow! That's really the *coup de grace* isn't it? That's really the *coup de grace*!" I like the Arkansan's response. "I don't know what you call them in Boston, but out here in Arkansas, we just call them hot tubs!"

Do you enjoy being around common folks? I know people who are comfortable with who they are, and have no need to impress. They don't put on airs or wear masks. And yet somehow, in their honesty and in their simple humanity, there's something remarkably strong and refreshing.

It's the same with children, and I believe that's what Jesus was talking about when he told his disciples that if they did not become as little children, they would never enter the kingdom of Heaven. We enter the kingdom by childlike faith and trust. And we live in the kingdom with that same childlikeness, trusting God—believing that God is going to do what God says. If we have this kind of childlikeness, we live in openness, and that means we are ready for surprises.

But our culture mitigates against that kind of childlike openness. Most of us live our lives braced against surprise.

I came across a phrase recently that really grabbed my imagination. It was a phrase that the singer Mary Martin used to describe her grandmother. She said her grandmother lived in a state of "incandescent amazement." No wonder Mary Martin's grandmother lived to be ninety-nine. Incandescent amazement—the mark of childlikeness—finding the world interesting, astonishing, surprising, and enjoying every minute of it. Open to the world—trusting God—that's childlikeness, and we don't want to give that up.

When Paul had shared his "hymn of love," he suggested that growing in love is the mark of maturity. His image was that of "becoming an adult" and "putting away childish things."

We need to make the distinction between *childish* and *childlike*. Childishness is the mark of immaturity; childlikeness is a sign of wholeness. Love is in conflict with and calls us out of childishness. Childlikeness is the spirit in which love grows.

Reflecting and Recording

Jesus called us to become as a little child if we would enter the kingdom. He used the word *receive*. "Whoever does not receive the kingdom of God as a little child will never enter it" (Luke 18:17).

Receiving the kingdom, I take it, means living in it. I suggest four marks for receiving and living in the kingdom.

One: having the capacity to wonder;
Two: being capable of spontaneity;
Three: being comfortable with self;
Four: being committed to change.

Love is who Jesus was. Love is what Jesus was all about. More than any other word, love describes the dynamics of the kingdom. The kingdom of God is the kingdom of love. The marks of receiving the kingdom are repeated here. Take some time reflecting on each. Make notes about how loving and being loved is a part of each.

Having the capacity to wonder

Being capable of spontaneity

Being comfortable with self

Being committed to change

Spend a few minutes asking yourself, "In what areas do I need to grow?"

During the Day

Be especially attentive to children today. What do they teach you about growth, love, and the kingdom?

GROUP MEETING FOR WEEK SIX

Introduction

This meeting and the next are the last planned group meetings. At this one, your group may want to discuss the future. Would you like to stay together for a longer time? Are there books, tapes, and so forth you would like to use corporately? If you're part of the same church, is there a way you might share the experience with others in the church?

Sharing Together

1. Let the leader open with prayer, or call on someone else to do so (consult that person ahead of time), then sing a chorus or hymn everyone knows.

2. Invite two or three volunteers to share an experience or relationship of loving in a way that made a difference in someone else's life.

3. Spend eight to twelve minutes talking about the "covering" dimension of love.

4. Invite two or three volunteers to share experiences when they knew they were *carried* by the love of Christ or the love of another.

5. Spend the balance of your time discussing the question, "How many times do you take the prodigal back?" Deal with the issue of "tough love."

Praying Together

1. On Day Five you named persons you know who are "in the far country." Refer to that and give persons the opportunity to name any of these persons, with someone in the group praying for each person as he/she is named.

2. Now allow any person in the group to ask for special prayer. As a need is mentioned, let the group pray silently or let someone offer a verbal prayer in response. Continue until all needs are prayed for.

3. Close by inviting the entire group to pray about direction for the group which will be decided at the next group meeting; then share together the Lord's Prayer.

WEEK SEVEN

Some Tough Issues

LOVE AND SACRIFICE

If I give away all my possessions, and if I hand over my body
so that I may boast, but do not have love, I gain nothing.

—1 Corinthians 13:3

A LIFE SACRIFICED FOR ANY OTHER MOTIVE than love is wasted.

I know a woman whose husband divorced her when they were in
their early fifties. They had married young and had had three children in
the very early years of their marriage.

The children were all grown and had left home. The husband
abused her mentally, sexually, and in other physical and emotional ways.

After the divorce, the woman moved into the home with her
parents. It was a mutual decision. She was their oldest child, born when
her parents were eighteen years old. They were healthy, and delighted to
be able to share their home. She was economically insecure, but also felt a
duty to care for her parents, since she now had no husband and her
children were on their own.

This woman became a victim of her own decision and will. She lived
a martyr's life of what she would call sacrifice. She became bitter and
sad. All joy—even the capacity for joy—seemed annulled.

I had the funeral of an eighty-year-old woman a few months ago.
Five years before, I had had the funeral of her ninety-five-year-old
mother. Eighty-year-old Frances was one of the happiest, most joyful
women I have known. Her husband died when she was sixty, the same
year her father died. She and her mother moved in together and shared a
home for fifteen years. She literally gave her life to her mother.

It may be simplistic, but the difference was obvious to me. One
woman sacrificed out of duty, another out of love. Sacrifice is a noble
commitment. But sacrifice without love is barren, destructive, drains all

138

joy, and, according to Paul, counts for nothing.

Jesus said, "Greater love has no man than this, that a man lay down his life for his friends" (John 15:13, RSV). Don't miss what he was saying. He was not absolutizing sacrifice, nor was he defining love only in terms of sacrifice. Much is said about sacrifice in religion. In fact, the most primitive religions make their offerings—their sacrifices—to placate or bribe their gods. Michael Harper reminds us that

> Saul, that most carnal of Jewish kings, tried this one on the prophet Samuel when he told him that he had preserved some of the Amalekite cattle and sheep, "to sacrifice to the Lord our God." But Samuel was having none of that. His answer was devastating: "Has the Lord as great delight in burnt offerings and sacrifices as in obeying the voice of the Lord? *Behold, to obey is better than sacrifice,* and to hearken than the fat of rams" (1 Sam. 15:22). In other words sacrifice is all right provided it is done in obedience to the Lord: sacrifice is not acceptable to God in the place of obedience. Obedience to God is absolute, sacrifice is always relative to it (Harper, pp. 35-36).

Love of God issues in obedience to God. That obedience may call for sacrifice of different sorts, and has in numerous instances throughout history called for sacrificial death. What it always calls for is death to self, which we will consider more tomorrow.

Reflecting and Recording

Remembering the stories of the two women and their sacrifice, think of persons you may know who have sacrificed on behalf of others. List them under these designations:

Sacrifice out of Duty   **Sacrifice out of Love**

Spend some time thinking about these persons. This is not a clear-cut issue. Some persons do find meaning or some degree of joy in sacrificing out of duty. But is there a qualitative difference between those who sacrifice out of love, and those who do so out of duty?

Ponder these questions:

Can love and duty be combined in a calling upon our life, or as a motivation for a particular "sacrifice"?

In your own life, are you doing some things out of duty which you need to baptize with love?

During the Day

Remember that the call is not to refuse duty, but to *infuse duty with love.*

Day Two

LOVE, SELF-DENIAL, AND SELF-AFFIRMATION

JESUS WAS RATHER CLEAR ABOUT IT: "Those who find their life will lose it, and those who lose their life for my sake will find it" (Matt. 10:39). That's not the only way he said it. "If any want to become my followers, let them deny themselves and take up their cross daily and follow me" (Luke 9:23).

If it is possible for a command of Jesus to be tougher for one age than for another, then ours is the age for which this particular Jesus-call is toughest. Christopher Lasch, in his best-selling book, designates ours as *The Culture of Narcissism* (Warner Books, 1983). Some called the 1970s "the narcissistic decade" and the 1980s the decade of "me-ism."

Jesus did say that we are to "love our neighbor as ourselves," and it is easy to conclude that if we don't love ourselves, we can't love our neighbor. The issue is not whether we are to love ourselves but how easy it is for self-love to become a sinful, self-crippling, other-destroying narcissism.

In the 1960s I became somewhat caught up in the human-potential movement with its emphasis on self-actualization. I believe, with Dr. Paul Vitz, that that whole human potential movement, with its emphasis on self-actualization and self-realization, in many ways went to an extreme and produced what he titled his book, *Psychology as Religion: The Cult of Self-Worship* (Eerdmans, 1977).

It's not easy to keep a healthy balance. *Agape*, the love Jesus incarnated and calls for, is essentially love of others. Yet, he did say we are to love others as we love ourselves. So there must be some legitimate self-love. But does this mean that love of God is the first commandment of Jesus, love of neighbor the second, and love of self the third?

Some would argue yes. And they have good support for this in the "condition" of people. Some of the most tragic human situations with which I have dealt as a pastor have been instances which involved, in the extreme, destructive self-hate. To a lesser extreme that falls short of radical self-destructiveness are all the expressions of low self-worth and lack of self-esteem. I've known countless persons who, at least in the way they have lived their lives and have expressed themselves in relationships, have needed to see self-love as a commandment. My overly-enthusiastic response to the human potential movement, which I confessed earlier, was rooted in my deep need for affirmation, for a genuine experience and feeling of self-worth.

What we must not ignore is the mirror side of this issue of self-love: the natural condition that can so easily be the perversion of our will to self-centeredness, selfishness, and sin. Much of what is wrong in society and in our own individual relationships is rooted in a perversion of, or an undisciplined, self-love.

That is the reason *agape*, and none of the other kinds of love (*eros, storgē, philia*) is our measure for loving the Jesus way. When *agape*, willful caring for the sake of others, is dominant in our lives, self-love is disciplined and finds meaning in "seeking not its own." This is not easy, but we can do it. We can love ourselves *selflessly*, rather than *selfishly*. When we love ourselves selflessly, we can love others in the same way. And that *selfless* love of self and of others provides the ultimate self-affirmation. We are affirmed by Christ who loves us, and who is pleased that we have discovered his way of living with meaning. "Give and it will be given you."

Reflecting and Recording

Spend some time reflecting on the following:

Would we be better off to cease talking about self-love, and talk instead about self-worth?

To get a better understanding and direction for living as it relates to love, self-love, and self-worth, would it be better to think and talk in terms of self-mastery rather than self-realization?

Would it be helpful to think about love for self's sake as self-love—which is unhealthy and destructive—and to think about love of self for God's sake and for the sake of others as self-acceptance—which is healthy and harmonizes with Jesus' command to love our neighbor as ourself?

In loving self, how can we be self-affirming without being self-asserting in "seeking our own way"?

During the Day

Be alert today to whether your love of self expresses itself *selfishly* or *selflessly*.

Day Three

LOVE AND FIDELITY

He answered, "Have you not read that the one who made them at the beginning 'made them male and female,' and said, 'For this reason a man shall leave his father and mother and be joined to his wife, and the two shall become one flesh'? So they are no longer two, but one flesh. Therefore what God has joined together, let no one separate."

—Luke 19:4-6

I WAS SHOCKED. I WAS TAKING MY SEAT IN THE AIRPLANE when I saw it lying where a passenger had left it. *Time* magazine, August 15, 1994. It was a dramatic cover, enough to attract anyone's attention. Stark against a black background, in big white letters, was printed the word INFIDELITY, and underneath this the caption, "It may be in the genes." Above all this was a broken wedding ring, severed in two places.

This dramatic cover announced the lead article, entitled "Our Cheating Hearts," by Robert Wright, adapted from his book *The Moral Animal: Evolutionary Psychology and Everyday Life* (Pantheon, 1994). The premise of evolutionary psychology is that the human mind, like any other organ, was designed for transmitting genes to the next generation. Thus the shocking magazine cover suggesting that infidelity may be in our genes.

I don't know enough about evolutionary psychology, anthropology, or any science of genetics. On the surface, it may certainly appear that infidelity is in our genes. We can let the scientists deal with *how* this may be true, but we can't disregard the prominence of infidelity in our current culture. At least one out of every two marriages in America is ending in divorce, and adultery—infidelity in marriage—is a destructive factor in human relations.

One dramatic fallout of divorce and broken homes is seldom considered. "In combing through 1976 crime data, [Martin] Daly and [Margo] Wilson found that an American child living with one or more substitute parents was about 100 times as likely to be fatally abused as a child living with biological parents. In a Canadian city in the 1980s, a child age two or younger was 70 times as likely to be killed by a parent if living with a stepparent and a natural parent than if living with two natural parents" (*Time*, August 15, 1994, p. 51).

I was surprised that the *Time* article moved to the question of morality, and I was impressed with the concluding paragraph: "We have at least the technical capacity to lead an examined life: self-awareness, memory, foresight, and judgment. Still, chronically subjecting ourselves to moral scrutiny and adjusting our behavior accordingly is hardly a reflex. We are potentially moral animals—which is more than any other animal can say—but we are not naturally moral animals. The first step to being moral is to realize how thoroughly we aren't" (Ibid., p. 52).

Infidelity is the result of undisciplined *eros*-love. When marriages get tough, when our partners are no longer "attractive" to us, when our "impulses of wanderlust" emerge, and the deadly idea that we married the wrong person comes to mind, if our commitment to *agape* love is not renewed and kept strong, we will surrender to the "natural impulses," as though they were *in our genes* and as though we had no control over them.

What is "natural" and/or what is in our genes is not the way we are called to live by Christ. The new life that can be ours in him is grounded in *agape*-love, which is our very best weapon in the battle against sexual promiscuity and infidelity.

Reflecting and Recording

This day's concern could be for you the most relevant or the most irrelevant of this workbook journey. I offer no guidance for your reflection, except to urge you to give this concern its due.

During the Day

For those who are married: offer signs of *agape* love and commitment to your spouse.

For both the unmarried and married: though we have concerned ourselves today with sexual infidelity or infidelity in marriage, there are other expressions of infidelity. Guard against these today.

$$\boxed{\textit{Day Four}}$$

LOVE AND THE CHURCH— A COMMUNITY OF COMPASSION

COMPASSION IS LOVE IN ACTION, a primary expression of *agape*. The Epistle of James sounds the call clearly:

> If a brother or sister is naked and lacks daily food, and one of you says to them, "Go in peace; keep warm and eat your fill," and yet you do not supply their bodily needs, what is the good of that? . . . You see that a person is justified by works and not

by faith alone. Likewise, was not Rahab the prostitute also justified by works when she welcomed the messengers and sent them out by another road? For just as the body without the spirit is dead, so faith without works is also dead.

—James 2:15-16, 24-26

Elizabeth O'Connor, in her book *The Eighth Day of Creation*, tells of an experience of St. Francis de Sales:

St. Francis de Sales was once approached by a disciple who said to him, "Sir, you speak so much about the love of God, but you never tell us how to achieve it. Won't you tell me how one comes to love God?" And St. Francis replied, "There is only one way and that is to love Him." "But you don't quite understand my question. What I asked was, 'How do you engender this love of God?'" And St. Francis said, "By loving Him." Once again the pupil came back with the same question, "But what steps do you take? Just what do you do in order to come into the possession of this love?" And all St. Francis said was, "You begin by loving and you go on loving and loving teaches you how to love. And the more you love, the more you learn to love" (O'Connor, pp. 66-67).

In our effort to love the Jesus way, and to keep on loving that we might learn more to love, we need a community of love to support us in our commitment. We also need to share with the community as we seek to make a love impact on the places where we live.

At her best, the church is that—a community of compassion. Matthew Fox, in *A Spirituality Named Compassion* (Winston Press, 1971), says that "compassion is not knowing about the suffering and pain of others. It is, in some way, knowing that pain, entering into it, sharing it and tasting it insofar as that is possible." We are not simply called to know that others suffer, to assess the painful situation in which they may be; we are to *feel* the other's feelings. And not only to feel the other's feelings, but to act on behalf of the other."

I have been a minister for forty-two years. Thirty-two of those years I have been pastor of a local congregation. I am convinced that a congregation cannot be true to the calling of Jesus Christ apart from an intentional effort to minister to the poor and other marginalized and/or oppressed people in our communities. Though we won't explore this notion broadly in this workbook, let's simply focus for a moment on the poor. Let me sound two warnings. First, we must not idolize the poor to the point of making them sinless, perfect beings. The poor and the rich are both sinners in need of reconciliation to God. The poor do not automatically qualify for the kingdom of God, any more than anyone else. As Theodore Williams said in an address to the Sixteenth World Methodist Conference in 1991,

> While we must do all we can to see that the poor find liberation from oppression, poverty, hunger and sin, we must remember that we cannot bring in the Utopia of perfect justice and peace. Though we believe in the present reality of the kingdom of God in our midst, we also believe in its future realization when there will be perfect justice and peace and there will be no poverty, hunger and oppression.

The second warning I would sound is this: We must resist the tendency to institutionalize our concern for the poor. We've done too much of that already. Again, Williams says,

> We build hospitals to express our concern for the sick, orphanages to express our concern for the orphans, homes for widows to express our concerns for the widows and hand over our responsibility to these institutions absolving ourselves of costly personal involvement. These institutions have grown independently from the church and have lost the original sense of mission. In many places they have become institutions for the elite and do not cater to the poor. In the hands of a few power mongers they have often become centers of injustice and exploitation.

Too often, the involvement of the church with the poor is not unlike that of a philanthropist handing out charity. We must change this. The concern must be expressed in personal involvement, in the spirit of servanthood.

When we do this corporately as a congregation, the church becomes a community of compassion—not only for the poor, but for others as well who know pain and suffering.

Reflecting and Recording

In his clear and challenging word about the Last Judgment, Jesus said,

Then the king will say to those at his right hand, "Come, you that are blessed by my Father, inherit the kingdom prepared for you from the foundation of the world; for I was hungry and you gave me food, I was thirsty and you gave me something to drink, I was a stranger and you welcomed me, I was naked and you gave me clothing, I was sick and you took care of me, I was in prison and you visited me."

—Matthew 25:34-36

Jesus was calling for *direct action* as did James in the scripture quoted earlier. Use the columns below to make a list of needs and opportunities for direct actions of compassion in your community—for you personally and for your church.

Personal   **Church**

Spend some time reflecting on where you and your church are in your work of compassion.

♥

During the Day
Seek to perform at least one act of compassion today.

Day Five

LOVE AND THE CHURCH: A PLACE OF HOSPITALITY

Let mutual love continue. Do not neglect to show hospitality to strangers, for by doing that some have entertained angels without knowing it.

—Hebrews 13:1-2

FELLOWSHIP IS AT THE HEART OF WHAT THE CHURCH IS ABOUT. In the church, we belong. We belong to Christ. Because we belong to Christ, we belong to one another. This means that the church, at her best, is a place of welcome, a place of hospitality. What a practical, impossible-to-miss expression of the love of Christ.

I had served Christ United Methodist Church in Memphis, Tennessee, for twelve years when I answered the call to become the president of Asbury Theological Seminary. After making the announcement, my wife and I began to receive letters from the congregation and from across the city, outside the congregation. The letters that meant the most to me were those which told how the congregation had been a source of love and life. Over and over again, persons would say, in one way or another, "This church has been Christ to me."

A young man who has fought a battle with homosexuality is being healed. He's finding the power to leave that lifestyle behind—in fact, he's on the verge of marriage. Some lines in the letter captured the depth of his gratitude. "Thank you—you knew, and yet you loved me. Thank this congregation. They didn't know, but had they known, I believe they would have loved me just the same. Christ is present here."

A young woman wrote: "I'm a member of your church but you probably don't know me. I joined about six months ago. I want you to know my story before you leave and I want you to know the power of this church." She poured out her story—five pages. Alcoholism, a broken marriage, two children now entering their teens, desperate economic conditions, hopelessness, no will to live . . . a tragic picture. "Perceptions," a TV and radio ministry, brought her to the church. The singles ministry, a growth group, our recovery ministry—all combined to make the witness, to communicate the fact which she expressed in just four words, "I found Christ here."

What had happened? These persons had experienced the love of Christ because our congregation was a place of hospitality. How many angels whom we may never know do we entertain when we show hospitality with the love of Christ?

Reflecting and Recording

There are many persons to whom the church needs to show hospitality. There are single parents and homosexuals, as I mentioned above. There are a number of recovering people in every community in America, persons recovering from all sorts of addictions. There are persons being released from jail and prison, homeless people, and the list goes on.

In your reflection yesterday, did you designate some needs and opportunities for compassion, a response to which might be hospitality?

Spend some time thinking about hospitality as your ministry and the ministry of your church.

♥

During the Day

Don't miss any opportunity to entertain angels.

Day Six

THORNY QUESTIONS

So if anyone is in Christ, there is a new creation: everything old has passed away; see, everything has become new!

—2 Corinthians 5:17

ONE OF THE CHARACTERISTIC PHRASES OF PAUL in the New Testament is *in Christ*. As in the scripture above, this was Paul's definition of a Christian, a person in Christ. It is interesting that Paul does not tell about his Damascus Road experience in descriptive detail. Luke records that dramatic event in the Acts of the Apostles. Paul himself doesn't recount an outward description of the experience—being struck down by a blinding light and hearing the voice of Christ. Rather, he talks about the *meaning* of that experience, and almost sings about it in exulting joy: "I have been crucified with Christ; it is no longer I who live, but Christ who lives in me; and the life I now live in the flesh I live by faith in the Son of God, who loved me and gave himself for me" (Gal. 2:20, RSV).

Jacopone da Todi (1230-1306) was an Italian poet and ascetic who defined a *saint* as "one in whom Christ is felt to live again." I believe that we could deal with the thorny questions which confront us regularly with stronger conviction, and respond with loving action, if we kept Paul's understanding of the Christian life (*in Christ*) and da Todi's definition of a saint (one in whom Christ is felt to live again) clearly in mind.

Since we can't deal with all these thorny issues in this workbook (that would require an entire book) we can at least list a few to offer a challenge as you draw near the end of this workbook journey.

Abortion: Over ten million babies have been killed by abortion in the past decade. This is an ongoing silent holocaust in our land. A number of doctors who perform abortions have been shot.

The Death Penalty: Test whether your feelings about the death penalty are consistent with your feelings about abortion.

Money: Money may be used as the most glaring expression of selfish self-love, or as one of the clearest witnesses of selfless love. It is one of the most powerful tools in our possession.

Penal Systems: It takes more money to keep an inmate in prison than it does to attend a first-rate university. $16,000 keeps a person locked up for one year; $80,000 builds the cell in which he is locked. No one today argues convincingly that any sort of significant rehabilitation is taking place in prison, and one wonders whether there are not more creative and redemptive ways to make restitution to the victims of crime.

We could expand the list: care for the aging, hunger, world peace, child abuse, the handicapped, literacy, justice reform, human rights. These are thorny issues with no easy answers—in fact, there often seems to be no answers. The Christian, however, cannot disregard them. If we are going to be persons "in whom Christ is felt to live again," then how we grapple with these complex issues is a number one priority.

Charles Colson gives dramatic testimony in his book *Transforming Society*:

When I was serving time for my part in the Watergate conspiracy, Al Quie, a senior congressman, offered to serve the remainder of my prison sentence if authorities would release me so I could be with my then-troubled family. Al, who later became governor of Minnesota, was a respected political leader; I was a member of the disgraced Nixon staff and a convicted felon. Al and I had not even been friends until a few months earlier when we met in a prayer group. Why would a man like Al Quie make such an offer?

The answer? Al took seriously Jesus' words: "As I have loved you, so you must love one another." This commandment is a central law of the Kingdom, and Al Quie was my first encounter with it.

One of the most transforming worldwide prison ministries and penal justice reform efforts has come from that radical expression of love by Al Quie.

Reflecting and Recording

The following is a list of many thorny issues that confront us and demand a loving response—what we would call a kingdom response. Live with this list for a while. Make some notes about responses that you are making and/or that your church may be making. Also make some notes about how you feel and what you would like to see done:

Care for the aging

People with handicapping conditions

Child abuse

Young women pregnant outside marriage

Abortion

Money

Penal systems

Human rights and other justice issues

World peace

Literacy

The death penalty

Hunger

Minorities

Victims of crime

Do you need to talk about some of these issues with some group in your church or an organization in your community?

During the Day
Don't let this day pass without doing something, however simple, that will cause someone to think of you as a person "in whom Christ is felt to live again."

| Day Seven |

WE KNOW IN PART

Love never ends. But as for prophecies, they will come to an end; as for tongues, they will cease; as for knowledge, it will come to an end. For we know only in part, and we prophesy only in part; but when the complete comes, the partial will come to an end. When I was a child, I spoke like a child, I thought like a child, I reasoned like a child; when I became an adult, I put an end to childish ways. For now we see in a mirror, dimly, but then we will see face to face. Now I know only in part; then I will know fully, even as I have been fully known. And now faith, hope, and love abide, these three; and the greatest of these is love.

—1 Corinthians 13:8-13

Paul certainly caught the attention of the Christians at Corinth when he wrote: "for now we see in a mirror dimly." Corinth was famous as a mirror manufacturing center. Its mirrors were known the world over, but its mirrors were, at best, poor by our modern standards. The modern mirror, as we know it with its perfect reflection, was not made until the thirteenth century. The mirrors of Corinth were highly polished metal, which gave a very poor reflection. The images seen in them were blurred and indistinct.

So Paul's word would have attracted the attention of the Christians at Corinth—the promise that one day all the images of life that were blurred, and all the images of God that were poorly formed—would one day be done away with, and we would fully see and fully understand.

What a promise! Now we know in part—but then we will know as we are known.

The love that will last forever is a love that comes through Jesus Christ and will be perfected in eternity.

Here is a story that hints at this promise:

A young man experienced the tragic death of his wife. Among other things, he was left with their small son to raise. The night after they got home from the cemetery, they went to bed early, as there was nothing else this young man could bear to do. As he lay there in the darkness, grief-stricken, heartbroken, and almost numb with his sorrow, his little boy broke the silence. "Daddy," he said, "where's Mommy?"

The father tried to get the little fellow to go to sleep, but the questions kept coming. "Where's Mommy? Why isn't she here? When is she coming back?"

The young father got up, went and got his little boy, and brought him to bed with him. The child was still disturbed, and occasionally would ask another probing and painful question. In one of those poignant moments that can only be explained as spirit-driven, the little boy reached out through the darkness and placed his hand on his father's face. "Daddy," he said, "is your face toward me?" When the father said that it was, and the little boy could feel it, he said the sweetest thing. "Daddy, if your face is toward me, I think I can go to sleep now." And in a few moments, he did!

This is a beautiful story, giving lead to the most helpful truth we can know. In Jesus, God turned his face toward us. In Jesus, we see what love means. And someday that knowledge will be even more complete. That's what Paul is saying. *One day we will know even as we are known.*

All the blurred images will one day come into clarity. All of the mystery will be revealed, so there is a continuity of love that stretches forward into eternity.

Paul Tillich was asked after his lectures on eternal life: "Explain to me what all these notes I've taken on your lectures mean." Tillich responded, "Look, all it means is God is going to win."

So he will—and the love and mercy and grace of God which we now know only in part, will be fully known.

And won't that be something! To see Jesus face to face. To be reunited with those we love—those whose memory we celebrate.

Tennessee Williams, the playwright, once said "Snatching the eternal out of the desperately fleeting is the great magic trick of human existence." Williams was right—but he was also wrong. It's not a magic trick. It's a commitment of faith to a life of love. That's what Paul is saying: "In this life we have three lasting qualities—faith, hope, and love. But the greatest of these is love" (PHILLIPS).

Reflecting and Recording

Spend as much time as you can during this period reflecting on this six-week workbook journey—the new insights that have come, the challenges and questions, the commitments you have made, the relationships that have been altered, the meaningful relationships you have experienced in your group, the enhanced awareness of the love you receive, the awareness of your need to be loving, and so forth.

Write a prayer of thanksgiving and commitment, reflecting where you are in your journey of learning to love the Jesus way.

During the Day

And in the days ahead, "Let love be genuine," and experience this amazing phenomenon: through our love, Christ's love is perfected. The First Epistle of John says it this way: "If we love one another, God lives in us, and his love is perfected in us" (1 John 4:12).

GROUP MEETING FOR WEEK SEVEN

Introduction

This is the final meeting designed for this group. You may have already talked about the possibility of continuing to meet. You should conclude those plans. Some groups find it meaningful to select two or three weeks of the workbook to go through again as an extension of their time together. Others continue for an additional set time, using other resources. Whatever you choose to do, it is usually helpful to determine the actual time line so that the group members can make a clear commitment.

Another possibility that has been very effective in the congregation I have served is for one or two persons to decide they will recruit and lead a group of new persons through this workbook. Many people are looking for a small-group growth experience. This can be a way to respond to that need.

Sharing Together

1. Invite one or two persons to share experiences of persons they know (maybe themselves) who have sacrificed out of duty and out of love. Talk for five minutes about the difference.
2. Spend ten to fifteen minutes talking about self-affirmation. What forms of self-love are good? destructive? How do we love ourselves selflessly? Why do we need the love of others, even when we know God loves us, in order to feel self-worth? What are the positive and negative dimensions of self-assertion?
3. Spend ten to fifteen minutes discussing the ministries of the church represented in your group as these ministries reflect the church as a community of compassion and a place of hospitality.

4. Invite two or three volunteers to share their experiences of bringing love to bear on one of the "thorny" issues listed on Day Six. It may be their own doing, how they have seen others act, or a first-hand knowledge of church response.

5. During the balance of your time, share about your experience during this six weeks. Verbalize your feelings, the insights that have come, the lessons, the discoveries. Reflect together on where you were and where you are now in your journey to love the Jesus way.

Praying Together

1. Begin your time of prayer by asking each person to briefly express gratitude to God for something significant that has happened to him or her as a result of these seven weeks.

2. Give each person an opportunity to share whatever decision or commitment he or she has made, or will make, concerning loving the Jesus way. It is important that these be specific. Follow each person's verbalizing of these decisions and commitments by having another person in the group offer a brief prayer of thanksgiving and support for that person.

3. A benediction is a blessing or greeting shared with another, or by a group, in parting. The "passing of the peace" is such a benediction. You take a person's hand, look into his or her eyes, and say, "The peace of the Lord be with you," and the person responds, "And may the Lord's peace be yours." Then that person, taking the hands of the person next to him or her, says, "The peace of the Lord be with you," and receives the response, "And may the Lord's peace be yours." Standing in a circle, let the leader "pass the peace," and let it go around the circle.

4. Having completed the passing of the peace, speak to one another in a more spontaneous way. Move about to different persons in the group, saying whatever you feel is appropriate for your parting blessing to each person. Or you may simply embrace the person and say nothing. In your own unique way, "bless" each person who has shared this journey with you.

NOTES

Barclay, William. *New Testament Words*. Philadelphia: Westminster Press (1974): 20-21.

Cronin, A. J. *Adventures in Two Worlds*. New York: McGraw-Hill Book Company, Inc. (1952): 326-327, 324.

Duncan, Dennis. *Love, The Word That Heals*. Arthur James Ltd. (1981): 1, 23.

Flynn, Leslie B. *Dare to Care Like Jesus*. Wheaton, IL: Victor Books (1983): 11-12.

Fynn. *Mister God, This Is Anna*. New York: Ballantine Books (1974): 19.

Harper, Michael. *The Love Affair*. Grand Rapids, MI: Wm. B. Eerdmans (1982): 211, 96, 97, 69, 68, 35, 36.

Kamal, Mohamed. "Why Tar Arabs and Islam?" *New York Times* (Feb. 16, 1987).

McConnell, Calvin D. "Christmas Is Incarnational Love." *The Upper Room Disciplines* (Dec. 24, 1991): 370.

Neaves, Norman. "Christ Lives in Everything." Unpublished sermon (April 30, 1989).

Neaves, Norman. "The Bonds of Belonging." Unpublished sermon (May 13, 1989).

O'Connor, Elizabeth. *The Eighth Day of Creation*. Waco, TX: Word Books (1971): 66-67.

Ritter, Dr. William A. "How Many Times Do You Take the Prodigal Back?" Unpublished sermon (October 16, 1988).

Trotter, Mark. "Guerrilla Goodness." Unpublished sermon (February 23, 1992).

THE MAXIE DUNNAM WORKBOOK COLLECTION

The Workbook of Intercessory Prayer (UR382)

The Workbook on Spiritual Disciplines (UR479)

The Workbook on Becoming Alive in Christ (UR542)

The Workbook on Coping as Christians (UR581)

The Workbook on the Christian Walk (UR640)

The Workbook on Christians Under Construction and in Recovery (UR683)

The Workbook of Living Prayer (Twentieth Anniversary Edition) (UR718)

All workbooks may be ordered from The Upper Room by calling 1-800-972-0433 or may be purchased at Cokesbury Bookstores.

If I speak in the tongues of mortals and of angels, but do not have love, I am a noisy gong or a clanging cymbal. And if I have prophetic powers, and understand all mysteries and all knowledge, and if I have all faith, so as to remove mountains, but do not have love, I am nothing. If I give away all my possessions and if I hand over my body so that I may boast, but do not have love, I gain nothing.

—1 Corinthians 13:1-3

The Spirit of the Lord is upon me, because he has anointed me to bring good news to the poor. He has sent me to proclaim release to the captives and recovery of sight to the blind, to let the oppressed go free, to proclaim the year of the Lord's favor.

—Luke 4:18-19

From the cowardice that dares not face new truths,
From the laziness that is content with half-truths,
From the arrogance that thinks it knows all truths,
Good Lord, deliver me.

Kenyan Prayer

Love is patient; love is kind; love is not envious or boastful or arrogant or rude. It does not insist on its own way; it is not irritable or resentful; it does not rejoice in wrongdoing, but rejoices in the truth. It bears all things, believes all things, hopes all things, endures all things.

—1 Corinthians 13:4-7

"Love has no more of pride than light has of darkness; it stands and bears all its fruit from a depth and root of humility."

William Law

"Every closed eye is not sleeping,
and every open eye is not seeing."

Bill Cosby

"Practice random acts of kindness and senseless acts of beauty."